BECAUSE OF BIRDS

A True Story

Nancy Ortenstone

Wishing you all
the best,
Nancy

Nature comes calling in this beautiful, moving book that reminds us of the old stories of saints and mystics who learned to speak a language of animals. Ortenstone speaks the language of birds. She's no saint, but rather a very warm, very human mother with an uncanny ability to get messages from creatures she befriends in Mexico and Minnesota. Her artist's eye delights the reader with images from her garden, her dreams—reality as she perceives it. Deeply colorful and wise, it unravels the complexities of the human heart with the timeless simplicity of a story well told.

- Nor Hall, Author of *The Moon and the Virgin* and *Those Women*

Cover photos: Jonathan Hulsh

Interior photo: Don Wolf

Design: Stephanie Carnes

A portion of this book first appeared in The Utne Reader.

ISBN 978-1-48358-429-4

About the Author

NANCY ORTENSTONE is a painter as well as a writer. She lives with her husband, writer/painter Pierre Delattre, on Picuris Indian Reservation land in the Northern New Mexico mountains outside of Taos where they have a gallery, Ortenstone Delattre Fine Art, which is managed by their artist daughter, Carla O'Neal. Nancy's paintings can be seen on her website at www.ortenstone.com.

For Pierre, Carla and Jennifer

Table of Contents

CHAPTER 1

Bird in My Dream

In recent years my fiction writing had begun to insist on its own direction. For reasons I didn't fully understand at the time, my attention focused on birds. The more I wrote about fictional birds, the more I found real birds flying into my life. Often I had the distinct impression they were bringing messages for my books, but I was mostly unaware that they were also initiating major changes in me. Only now, while remembering my many experiences with birds, am I able to see clearly the gifts they gave to me.

Almost against my will, a bird kept appearing in my first novella. Each time I took him out of the book, he would insinuate himself again. Eventually he became Bird, an essential character in the story. A year later, I began writing about an ornithologist who goes through a series of transformations because of her relationship to birds. In this book, Bird became the narrator.

Once while feeling blocked with the writing, I decided to call forth Bird in a dream, hoping he might offer a solution. Even though I had paid close attention to my dreams for years, it had never occurred to me before to will a fictional character into a dream. I was surprised when a huge version of Bird appeared in my sleep that very night.

With his long spindly leg and claw foot, he pantomimed the turning of a key. "Unlock the door," he said. "All I have to do is pick up the pencil and put it in my beak."

Soon after, my husband Pierre and I decided to spend a few days at our friend's vacant cottage hoping it would give us new perspectives on our work. When we arrived at dusk, the night wind felt raw, so we kept all the windows closed in the tiny kitchen, and settled in on the bench beside the table to read. Since the cottage had no electricity, both of us huddled next to the white gas lantern. When we began to feel extremely drowsy, we attributed this to the long drive and carried the lantern and books to the bedroom where we tucked ourselves into bed to read. Even though the room was small and stuffy, it was too cold outside to open any windows.

With the lantern still burning, we quickly fell into deep sleep. Soon a hazy image of a human-sized Bird appeared in my dream. He tried desperately to tell me something but couldn't reach me with his voice.

Just when I began to feel as if I was being sucked into a region way beneath the realm of dreams, I vaguely heard Bird say, "I can't lift my head off the pillow."

My immediate impulse was to try to lift my own head. I couldn't. In a panic, I struggled to wake myself, but my body remained submerged. A battle took place between my will and my physical self as I tried to move my hand towards Pierre. It seemed forever before he stirred awake enough to share the realization that something was drastically wrong with both of us.

With great effort, we managed to roll our lugubrious bodies to the edges of the bed and drop onto the floor. Surprisingly, I felt no pain as I struck. Gasping for air, we crawled towards the door dragging our bodies like huge heavy carcasses behind us.

After a long struggle, I reached the door but couldn't coordinate my muscles to lift my arm. When Pierre actually grasped the doorknob, he didn't have the strength to turn it.
Knowing it was our last chance for survival, Pierre grabbed the doorknob again and swung the door open. A gust of fresh air caressed our faces. Out on the patio we lay spread-eagled breathing deeply the air that smelled sweeter than any air anywhere.

We realized later that, because we had kept all the windows closed in both rooms, the white gas lantern had consumed the oxygen.

If I had died that night, my novel would never have been written.

Because Bird was in the process of being created within my imagination, my life meant his life. I discovered that the creatures we give life to are as determined as we are to stay alive until they have lived out their story. Not only do they live for us, but at times we live for them.

* * *

Once the novel was finished, I began to realize that the most intriguing stories were not the fictional ones but rather those that occurred in my life. Because of my obsession with birds, synchronicity started happening and I began to have intense relationships with living birds: a Peking Duck, a mourning dove, a hummingbird, and a Great Blue Heron. They prepared me for when my daughters left home by teaching the lessons of letting go.

During the time I first tried to muster the courage and confidence to write these stories, I met Isaac Bashevis Singer who said, "Tell the story that only you can tell." This has been my mantra, my encouragement each time I veered from the path of writing the bird stories that I lived.

* * *

I can't forget that, in my childhood, there were years of feathers and blood.

CHAPTER 2

The Turkey Farm

I like to believe that my fascination with birds began while I was living in Mexico, but I know that far back in my past there were thousands of noisy ugly birds in Minnesota.

Fridley, a suburb, a half hour north of Minneapolis, is now overpopulated and bursting at the seams, but during the time I was growing up, it was still very rural. In the early 1920's, Fridley was a Scandinavian settlement where my grandparents' flourishing dairy farm was situated miles from another homestead. When my parents were married, they built their home right across the dirt road from the farm.

After my grandmother's brother used the farm as collateral to borrow money to pay off his gambling debts, my grandparents had to struggle. Finally, grandpa insisted that they get rid of the last few cows who were, according to him, always demanding attention and never bringing in much money. Instead, he wanted to buy a brood of turkeys who would be "seasonal." The spring that I was seven years old, grandpa sold the last of the cows and bought three hundred baby turkeys. Within a couple of years he had increased the flock to more than a thousand. He would feed them until early November of each year when all the turkeys would be killed and sold for Thanksgiving and Christmas dinners, except for the few that were tucked into the freezer for our family feasts.

Soon grandpa began to look somewhat like a turkey himself, with his hunched back, sunken eyes, and unshaven stubble growing from his face.

Regardless of whether it was winter or summer, he wore his greying long underwear and black wool trousers held up by thick suspenders. The snuff he chewed stained not only his teeth a brownish yellow, but also the corners of his mouth, and the inside of his lips.

* * *

Slowly, the tractor crept into the turkey pen with grandpa perched high on the seat while I straddled the feed sacks stacked on the flatbed. The terror of being chased by an entire flock of turkeys thrilled me.

When grandpa stopped the tractor to hoist down the feed sacks and fill the troughs, I swung a big stick at the turkeys who managed to scramble up onto the flatbed to peck at my legs.

Their pimply heads were hideously ugly. I didn't like to look at the fleshy protrusions that dangled from their foreheads and chins.

The turkeys quickly devoured their meal, and by the time they were scratching at the sand in peevish discontent, I was safe on grandpa's lap steering the big tractor back towards the gate.

* * *

My father hated the turkey business, but he had married into the family, and was expected to help out. Grandpa didn't concern himself with the fact that his daughter's husband already put in nine hours a day as the foreman at a machine shop.

I adored my father. Every winter he would build my sister and me a skating rink in the backyard and never complain when he had to hold me up under the arms and skate behind me until my ankles grew strong enough to carry me across the ice on blades. That was in the sweet silence of winter when all the turkeys were gone.

But in the summer there was no escaping the turkeys' hideous noise, unless I hiked the mile down the dirt road to Rice Creek. There the sound of bubbling water washed away the clamor of the farm and left me free for fantasies of the future.

From high in the branches of the poplar, where I spent many summer afternoons day-dreaming, the frantic gobbling of the turkeys could be heard. From inside the brown shingled house my father had built on the lot adjacent to my grandparents, I could still hear the turkeys' constant gobbling. Even while I was asleep, their noise echoed through my dreams.

* * *

One brilliant autumn day I opened the door of the cement-block building used to store the grain. The blue flower printed dress I was wearing was made from the cotton feed sacks. As I stood in the doorway, the sunlight flooding in from behind me caught the glint of the long silver blade on the knife in my father's hand.

At least fifty turkeys hung upside down, tied at the ankles by ropes wrapped around the rafters. While carefully avoiding the flailing wings, my father pried each turkey's beak open, then jabbed his weapon deep into its throat. Mother followed behind him, plucking the feathers while the jerking bird was still warm and bleeding. She knew that after the bird dies, its feathers cling to the body and are much more difficult to pluck.

The frantic turkeys splattered the granary walls and my parents with their blood. I had never before seen the slaughter. While I watched with fascinated horror, a drop of blood flew toward the doorway and stained the front of my dress.

After witnessing the killing, every time I went into the granary to get a few handfuls of oats to eat, I tried not to look at the blood-splattered walls. But I always ended up staring at them and wondering just how many turkeys altogether had been hung from their feet to meet a brutal death.

At seven, I believed that the thrill I took in the death of those hideous birds had to be a mortal sin. When I tried to tuck this sin away, it grew. Like some creature locked in the basement, it fed itself on whatever it could sink its teeth into. Soon I began to feel it chewing on my very soul.

CHAPTER 3

Under the Weeping Willow

The driveway that led from the gravel road to our house circled around a majestic weeping willow whose branches cascaded elegantly, like great strands of leafy hair. Beyond the driveway sat our house nestled among plum and pine trees.

Inside the circle created by the driveway, in every patch of earth that wasn't shaded by the old willow, my mother grew flowers of all kinds – zinnias, bachelor buttons, daisies, pansies, and marigolds. On a hot summer afternoon the perfect place to sit for hours was under the umbrella created by this glorious tree.

One day while walking to the creek, I found a dead robin and carried it home to bury it under the willow. Before setting the bird into the grave I had dug, I carefully placed it inside a glass jar. I screwed the lid on so tight, I couldn't open it again. I wanted to protect the robin from anything that tried to get at it.

Often, I wondered what became of us after we died, but no one could tell me. What do we look like as we rot? Do we shrivel up? Will the bird's feathers vanish or will they remain in the jar while everything else disintegrates? Was it my intention to dig up the bird one day to see for myself what happens?

A few days after I buried the robin, I found another dead bird and then another. Soon I was having a funeral under the willow tree almost every day. More and more often birds somehow managed to die where I would discover them. Did they like it that I sang a hymn while I put them into a jar? Did they all want an elaborate funeral? Did they know that if they died nearby, I would bury them? It was a good thing my mother did a lot of canning, because I needed a plentiful supply of jars. I smuggled them out of the fruit cellar one by one, and she never mentioned missing any.

Do birds watch us humans? Do they know who puts out the seed and who sits waiting with a slingshot in hand?

After a while I quit holding bird funerals with the hope that if I did they would stop dying in our yard. Soon other deaths distracted me. My father's hunting dog, who had been around since before I was born, was run over by the man who brought the turkey feed. Never before had I seen either of my parents cry. For years after that, whenever I was feeling sad, and my mother would ask me why I was crying, I would say, "Because Butchie died." I had this idea that in my family you could only cry when the dog died.

Soon the willow tree itself died. It was a sad day when this comforting presence was chopped down.

CHAPTER 4

The Bird Dog

One late October when my father went pheasant hunting in Southeastern Minnesota, not far from Rochester, he invited me to come along. I was nine years old at the time. Down the back roads he knew well from previous hunting trips, he drove us through a landscape ablaze with autumn leaves. When we arrived at a big cornfield, he stopped the car, got out to load his gun, and took his stance. Then he sent me running through the tall dry cornstalks to flush the pheasants. I raced down the entire length of a row with my arms extended, my hands thrumming each cornstalk as I passed it. Soon the frantic sound of fluttering wings could be heard, followed quickly by several blasts bellowing from my father's gun.

I never once looked up in the sky to watch the birds fall. When I reached the end of the cornfield, I ran back towards the car, down a different row, once again rustling the cornstalks. Together my father and I looked for the birds that had fallen. His memory of where they had dropped out of the sky was impressive, even though he did have to search patiently for one or two.

Soon I grew tired and returned to the car where I climbed in to sit propped up behind the steering wheel on an extra hunting jacket. I didn't look closely at the pheasants when he carried them to the car to put them in the trunk. I tried not to notice that these birds - unlike the turkeys - were stunningly beautiful.

When he got into the car, he handed me the keys as my reward for flushing the pheasants. Thrilled by the power I felt, I drove the old Chevrolet across the field and back down the gravel road to the highway.

As soon as we arrived home, my father opened the trunk and laid the pheasants out on the grass, then called to my mother to come see our bounty. That's when I took a good look at the birds I had helped to kill.

While sunlight glittered off the emerald green feathers on the males, the mottled designs on the feathers of the females revealed their more subtle beauty. Seeing these elegant birds lying limp on the grass never to fly again, made me suddenly feel sick in the pit of my stomach. I felt that same way again when my mother served a glazed pheasant for Sunday dinner. Because I refused even to taste it, there was a scene at the table.

Never again did I run through the cornfields as my father's bird-dog. He finally quit asking if I wanted to come along. Maybe he thought that when I was a little older, if he taught me how to shoot a gun, I would want to accompany him on his hunting trips.

* * *

The hard kick against my shoulder when I pulled the trigger, and the blast right next to my ear hurt; but the pleased look on my father's face when I took accurate aim and shattered the clay pigeon was well worth my pain.

I liked being his "boy" and felt proud that by the time I was twelve years old I could handle a 22 with skill. That was before I lost my 20/20 vision and had to get eyeglasses. That was before I traded my blue jeans and t-shirt for a pink dress to wear to the school sock-hop.

I loved it when my father called me "muscles" even though he could easily have wrapped his hand around any part of my skinny arm. Maybe because I always struck out while playing baseball, I especially wanted to shoot the tin can off the fence post to make him proud. Yes, I liked being my father's "boy" and for a while, when I was nine years old, I had even liked being his "bird dog."

* * *

I'd cover the Formica table top in the kitchen with several layers of newspapers and help my mother pull out the turkeys' innards. The gizzard fascinated me the most. When I'd cut it open to inspect what the turkey had eaten, invariably I would find a few pebbles mixed in with the ground-up grain. These pebbles were my proof of the turkeys' stupidity, cause enough for their horrendous deaths, or so I tried to believe.

I was twelve years old when grandpa died. During his last days, I was terrified when my mother asked me to go over to stay with him so grandma could come to our house to eat.

A sour-sweet odor wafted through their house; it smelled almost rancid. In total silence I sat in the living room on the edge of grandpa's upholstered chair, gripping the arms until the knuckles on my hands turned white. I prayed that he wouldn't wake up and need anything. When he did call for grandma, I ran in terror to get her without saying anything to him at all.

I remember the night my mother came home to tell us he had died. I sat in the window seat for hours staring at their driveway, waiting to see who would come to get the body. But no one came while I was watching.

At the funeral my very stoic grandmother flung herself on her husband in the open casket and begged him not to leave her. It was my father who gently gathered her into his arms and helped her sit down in the front pew.

After the funeral, she stayed at our house and wailed throughout the night. No one could explain death to me or tell me where it was that grandpa went. When I saw the casket, something felt right about my having buried birds in jars.

To everyone's relief, grandpa's death released our family from the turkey business. I tried to tuck the ghosts of all the dead turkeys into the corners of grandpa's casket before he was buried, along with my guilt for the pleasure I took in their deaths. But it couldn't be done. The memories of the turkey farm had etched themselves into my psyche.

CHAPTER 5

Five Chickens, a Duck and a Pheasant

Besides the turkeys, the only other birds in my childhood were five chickens, a duck, and a pheasant. At first I adored the fluffy peeping creatures that had been dyed pink and blue for Easter. But they grew quickly and tried to attack me every time I went into the chicken house to feed them. They had become too turkey-like for me. I gladly relinquished ownership of them to my older sister Cathy.

The duck was a different story. He was a marvelous companion. I think my mother had intended to raise him for a Sunday dinner and never guessed that I would become so attached to him. I named him Puddles because that spring it rained a lot and he loved to splash about in the water that accumulated in the driveway. When I went off to summer camp for a week, I returned home to discover that Puddles had bonded to my two year old sister Lori. He sat right beside her while she played in the sandbox and followed close behind her as she tottered about in the yard. He seemed to have forgotten who I was. It still upset me, however, when my mother gave him away that Autumn to be eaten.

The pheasant belonged to no one. Every winter for several years he came to visit. My father, standing in front of the kitchen window, would call out, "Look, Peg-leg Pete is back." We would gather around to watch this one-legged pheasant hop around in the snow looking for seed.

CHAPTER 6

The Crow

The turkeys were gone forever, and birds seemed to vanish from my life. Or probably, I no longer had a moment to notice them. Oh, from time to time, I still heard the haunting song of the whippoorwill, and occasionally watched a robin tugging at a worm in the yard. But I felt no connection to birds. Not until I had been married for seven years, to the boy I had met at fourteen, did a bird insist that I pay attention to him.

We were living in Tucson, Arizona at the time, and I should have left the marriage a couple of years earlier, but I was trying desperately to make it work. Jennifer was just a toddler, and Carla was only six. Because I grew up in the 50's, I believed that a woman should devote herself to her husband's talent. I had just spent the last six years working at hated secretarial jobs in order to support the family while he went to art school and graduate school. If I had opened my eyes, I might have seen that his psyche wasn't healthy enough to ever take on responsibility for his family.

One afternoon as I sat on the front porch with my muddled mind and broken heart, I tried to sort things out. Every time I tried to express how I felt to my husband, I couldn't utter a word.

While I was lost in thought, a big crow settled into the tree next to the house and began heckling me. I knew I should break free from the marriage to start my life again and somehow to create a healthy environment for the girls, but I lacked the courage.

From that day on, every time I sat out on the porch, the crow appeared to taunt me. Pretty soon Carla was drawing scary pictures of this bird and I was writing poems about him, until finally I interpreted his relentless cackling at me as a sign that I should leave.

I packed a suitcase and left the southwest desert to return with the children to Minnesota. There we began a new life, just the three of us.

CHAPTER 7

Yet Another Duck...

The first bird I noticed in Minnesota was a duck squatting on the frozen Mississippi River. He was patiently waiting for the first thaw, which we all thought would never come. Winter can't last forever we would say to one another with optimism, but everyone in Minnesota knew that it already seemed to have lasted longer than forever.

My parents were now living in a rambler on a hill right above the Mississippi River. They mentioned having seen an eagle in their yard and an owl that my mother said all the other birds ostracized and teased; but I didn't pay much attention. Nor did I ever watch to see who flew in to eat from the many feeders they had set up in their glorious yard. I was preoccupied with trying to put the pieces of my life back together and trying to mend my broken heart.

One day when I returned to their house, after registering at the university, my arms full with books, and my head full with questions about how I would manage taking care of the children, working to support us, and at the same time going back to school. No one was home. My mother had taken Carla and Jennifer shopping. I looked out the picture window and noticed the duck sitting on the frozen river.

"How do you do it?" I shouted through the window. "Just sit there so content waiting for the ice to melt?" I flung my books onto the floor and burst into tears. It was a rare occasion that I had such a chance to release my emotions. Usually, I struggled to maintain my composure in front of the children. And other times, when I wanted to express anger or despair, I didn't even know how.

It felt good to cry. When all my emotion was spent, I looked at the duck and vowed, "If you can do it, so can I." Within the week I had found a job, an apartment, and had started my studies at the university.

For another seven years there were no birds in my life. If any had flown close, I wouldn't have noticed them. I was too busy dealing with the constant task of survival.

I wonder what I would have thought on that day that I had identified with the duck out in the cold, if someone had told me that one day another duck would enter my life, and I would have my first intense nitty gritty love relationship with a bird.

CHAPTER 8

The Purple Finch

Seven years later on Easter Sunday, I was on the threshold of making a major change in my life. Pierre and I had recently met, and we were trying to decide whether or not we wanted our paths to merge. We knew that they already had but it seemed important to come to a conscious decision about it. I had neglected to do that earlier in my life, and consequently, had become caught up with my first husband's destiny instead of my own.

The children and I went to visit my parents who still lived beside the Mississippi River. After a lovely dinner, my mother, Jennifer and I went for a walk while Carla stayed behind to help my father in the garden.

About a mile up the river, we stopped to marvel at a gnarled old oak tree. Jenny climbed inside the huge hole in its trunk while my mother informed us that it was one of the oldest oaks in all of Minnesota.

Spring was just beginning to show itself, and all of life somehow seemed hopeful again. When we arrived at the part of the river that flowed in front of my parents' house, we found a purple finch lying dead on the ground. I suggested we bury it near the shore, but Jennifer adamantly demanded that we do so away from the river. I guess she wanted to protect it from the dark swirling water. We climbed the embankment at the edge of my father's rolling lawn, where we dug a shallow grave.

While Jennifer and I tied two twigs together with twine to make a cross, my mother told us how sorry she was that none of her tulips were yet in bloom.

As we patted the mound of earth over the purple finch's body, several birds flew in to land on a branch that extended out above our heads. A couple of sparrows, an Oriole, another purple finch and some other birds gathered and began singing. It was as if a whole chorus of birds had come to sing the purple finch's soul up out of the ground and back into the tree.

I felt that I had just buried my troubled past. Later I discovered that during the time we were holding the funeral for the finch, Pierre had been sitting beside the river, several miles upstream, struggling to make a decision about his future. He said that at one point all doubt suddenly vanished, and he knew that soon we would be sharing our lives.

Not long after this, while I was writing my first novella, Bird began to take form in my imagination. I felt as if I had come up out of the darkness and was just beginning to find my voice.

CHAPTER 9

Two Black Ravens

Pierre and I decided to sell everything we owned and move with my daughters to San Miguel de Allende, a small colonial town in central Mexico. I looked forward to having the time to devote myself to writing. I knew that the only way I would discover my own voice was by trying to express myself on paper. Writing had always been difficult for me. I felt blocked and sometimes would just sit and stare at the blank page unable for the longest time to put down the first word.

The landscape surrounding San Miguel reminded me of the Southwest desert but with an even more perfect climate. Coming from Minnesota, I always had to stop and figure out what time of year it was, because the sun shone every day, and the temperature was almost always pleasant. To my delight, I discovered that throughout the year San Miguel has flowers and birds in abundance.

With time every day to write, I kept up the struggle and soon finished my novella. Then I began writing about an ornithologist whose relationship to birds transforms her. It was all purely fiction at that point, because I had no recent life experiences with birds to write about.

Soon after we arrived in San Miguel, Pierre introduced me to two old friends, Carl and Lorena, who were busily at work on a book about camping in Mexico. We all shared the ache of sitting cramped behind a typewriter for hours on end. So several afternoons a week, after writing all day, Pierre and I would walk across town to soak in their hot tub.

On one of those delightful excursions, while Pierre was caught up in conversation with our friends in the kitchen, I slipped into the steaming tub alone, lay back and rested my head on the edge of the patio. Luxuriating in the calming water, I gazed at a clear blue sky, while all my muscles relaxed and my mind began to quiet.

Beside their house grew ancient pecan trees, the tallest trees I had ever seen. When the nuts fell, they dropped out of the sky like wooden stones to knock on their roof. These pecans were like constant gifts falling from heaven.

I looked beyond the pecan trees to study the cloudless sky and a bird flew into view. He was flying so high I couldn't see who he was. Traveling through endless blue, he appeared like a black speck. While watching him cross the sky, something that looked like a leaf appeared in my sight about twenty feet below him and began drifting down to earth.

As it floated towards the roof of the house, a breeze caught it and danced it towards the patio, until it settled on the water in the hot tub right beside me. When I picked it up, I realized it was a feather that had fallen from the bird I had been watching. I accepted this as a sign that birds and I were becoming connected in some mysterious way.

When Carl, Lorena, and Pierre dipped into the tub, I showed them the black feather that we all surmised must have belonged to a grackle. But the way it had come to me seemed anything but ordinary. This feather was the beginning of many more connections with birds. In fact, that very afternoon, Carl told me about two ravens at the market that I should buy myself as a birthday present.

"They're intelligent enough to train to talk," he told me. Because he had raised macaws for years, he was an authority on talking birds.

* * *

The very next day, Jennifer and I went to the market to see the ravens. I hadn't really thought about where I would keep them if we brought them home. I didn't believe that I could ever keep a bird in a cage and yet the idea of having birds of my own, especially ones I could teach to talk definitely intrigued me.

In a 5' x 10' cage at the market, among many smaller and more colorful birds, sat two huge shimmering black ravens. From a shit-covered stand where they perched side by side, these pointy-beaked birds returned our gaze.

They looked like two wizards who had been caught in their own mean-spirited magic. Jennifer and I quickly came to the same conclusion; we didn't want these demonic-looking characters in our lives.

CHAPTER 10

Far Out

"You bitch!" Lorena hissed at the macaw, who had just pierced her earlobe with its beak and flown back to perch on the edge of the feeder. The bird had gingerly stepped off the stand to curl her claws around Lorena's forefinger when suddenly all we saw was a blur of feathers, as it lunged at Lorena without warning. By the time Lorena had raised her hand to bash her attacker, the macaw, named Far Out, had already returned to her perch.

Lorena dabbed at the dripping blood and glared at the bird, daring her to strike again. But Far Out turned her head to stare in the opposite direction, feigning disinterest in Lorena's very presence.

"She's pissed," Lorena explained, "She has acted this way ever since we brought her and Arturo to live at the Villa."

I glanced around at the courtyard in the quaint colonial hacienda abundant with bougainvillea, potted geraniums and hanging baskets of fuchsia. Far Out's perch stood in the center of this lovely patio that the nine suites looked out upon.

This was the first time I had seen Far Out, although I had heard many stories about her and Arturo. When Lorena and Carl began writing their book on camping in Mexico they spent a lot of time traveling. That is when they decided their macaws would be better off staying at the Villa Santa Monica, which was owned by friends. They had no way of knowing that, almost as soon as the birds arrived, Sinbad, the toucan who already lived there, would want Arturo out of the way so he could have Far Out all to himself. When Arturo had been found dead one morning, everyone (except Carl and Lorena who suspected foul-play) assumed he had died of old age. He had lived for sixty years with a gypsy-like woman who sold him to Carl just before she died.

"Far Out's disposition completely changed when Arturo was gone. She blamed us," Lorena said to me. "Try singing her a song. If you could alter her bad mood, she might decide to sing for you."

I should sing to this angry bird, I thought to myself. What if she doesn't like my voice and goes for my eyes? I didn't trust her at all. In fact, I stayed at least ten feet away.

"I don't think I even know any songs," I said, stalling for time while I scrolled through my memory for the tunes my father and I used to sing during long car trips. What was that about Uncle Bill's goat tied to the railroad tracks?... Oh no, that was cruelty to animals. The bird wouldn't like that. How about 'Old Shep'?... No, it was too sad, and the dog got shot in the end. Before I even realized what I was doing I began belting out, "Someone's in the kitchen with Dinah... Someone's in the kitchen, I know-o-o-o..." And with abandon that surprised me, I sang the entire song. Before I even had the chance to feel good about having been able to let go of all inhibitions and throw myself into it, I heard the most heinous laughter coming from Far Out.

I felt humiliated. It was the ultimate experience of being laughed at. And after I had mustered enough bravado to sing in the first place. The intrigue that such laughter could come from a bird distracted me from feeling devastated.

"She liked that," I was surprised to hear Lorena say. "Look, you've enticed her to sing."

Far Out ruffled her feathers, tossed her head back just a bit, positioning herself like an opera singer on stage and sang in a perfect scratchy church twang, "Rock of ages, cleft for me..."

While I stood wondering which was more amazing coming from this bird, the sound of human laughter or the hymn, Lorena busily scratched Far Out's body where the little claw feet couldn't reach.

"I'll come to see you more often," Lorena promised Far Out. "Maybe Nancy will come sometimes too. She likes birds." I didn't dare confess that I was terrified of this particular bird, huge and bewildering as she was. In some way she stirred awake my old terror of the turkeys.

On the way home, Lorena told me Arturo and Far Out's history. Soon after Carl and she had bought Arturo, some hippies passing through town had sold them Far Out. Before falling madly in love with Arturo, all she ever said was, "Far Out, Far Out." It was Arturo who taught her how to imitate his previous owner's laugh. Gloria was an herbalist, a midwife, and sort of a Mexican version of a shaman. Everyone in her village believed that she had healing powers. The first time Carl and Lorena heard Arturo laugh they thought Gloria had been resurrected. Perhaps, in the bird, she had.

Lorena told me it was Carl who had taught both birds to sing the hymn. She also described how the macaws often acted like children. Whenever Carl and Lorena were totally absorbed writing their book, Arturo would start in, "Carl, Carrrrrl, Carrrrlllll," until it became impossible to concentrate. Then if Carl would ignore him, Far Out would start in calling sweetly, "Lorena, Lorena," until finally she'd screech out "Loreeeennnaaaaa," in a voice that sounded like she was dying. They would continue this harassment until Carl and Lorena were screaming at them to shut up, whereupon they would laugh the Gloria laugh until something was thrown at them.

"Gloria..." I slowly repeated the name out loud and excitedly explained to Lorena that it was the perfect name for the ornithologist in my new novel. For months I had been searching for her name. All I knew was that I wanted it to imply light and song. And to think her name had been given to me by a bird!"

"Maybe you'd like to keep Far Out," Lorena suggested.

"Me?"

I realized that Lorena must have had that in mind when she invited me to come along on her visit to the Villa.

"What could be better? While you're busy writing the bird novel, who knows what other revelations you would have with Far Out living at your house."

I gave her one excuse after another but never confessed that Far Out terrified me. I did promise that whenever Lorena had to go out of town, I would visit her amazing macaw.

She seemed satisfied for the moment.

CHAPTER 11

Gilguerro

To celebrate my birthday, Pierre and I walked down the cobblestone hill towards the center of town anticipating a lovely lunch at the elegant Sierra Nevada Restaurant. We stopped at the bank and withdrew 700 pesos. As we strolled across the plaza, we noticed a Mexican man standing on the corner beside several stacks of tiny wooden cages filled with birds of all kinds, colors and sizes.

When we walked over to take a closer look at the pretty little parakeets, each one a different combination of pastel colors, we noticed three large cages filled with cardinals. It was strange to see the birds associated with the pines in Minnesota being sold in the hot desert of Mexico. No doubt the vendor thought these rare birds with their macho crests and bright red feathers were a lucrative catch.

An American woman standing beside me explained, with indignation, that the cardinals had been captured at the Rio Grande River while migrating. My eye was drawn to a striking emerald-green bird, the size of a robin, who had a bright purple head and thick black circles around his eyes. Although I was attracted to such amazing colors, his big pointy black beak gave me pause.

Pierre surprised me by suggesting that instead of celebrating over an extravagant lunch, we buy a bird to keep in my study until I finished writing my novel. We had often commented on the Mexican's custom of decorating their patios with cages of songbirds and swore that we could never keep a bird in a cage. We were shocked to learn that the male sang most beautifully and ardently if he and the female were kept close to each other but in separate cages.

It amazed me that within minutes of hearing Pierre's suggestion, I was checking out all the birds, trying to decide which one to buy.

When I squatted down to get a better look at the birds in the lower cages, a somewhat plump thrush-sized grey bird noticed my gaze, threw back his head and warbled the most heart-rending song. I stood up to ask the vendor the price of the green-purple bird whose colors still intrigued me, but before he could answer '600 pesos,' I found myself once more looking at the grey bird.

As soon as the bird saw me peering in at him again, his throat began to ripple. He repeated his lovely song.

The third time I bent down to look at him and he began to sing, I knew without a doubt that he was singing for me. How could I resist such a soulful song? It didn't surprise me to be told that he cost 700 pesos, because I already felt that my connection to this bird was destined.

The vendor opened the door of the cage, poked his thick hand inside and wrapped his stubby fingers around the bird he called "Gilguerro." He pulled him out and stuffed him into a little brown paper bag with two slits in the side for air holes.

Gilguerro remained perfectly still and quiet during our walk to the tienda where Pierre and I pooled our spare change and bought a cage. All the way up the hill and into my study, we didn't hear a sound coming from the bag. But when I set Gilguerro into the cage, he began thrashing his wings and bashing his tail feathers against the bars. He would hop up onto the perch, spread his wings, leap off and in the process fray his feathers. He spilled his water and scattered sesame seeds all over the new stack of writing paper on my desk.

In an attempt to calm him and coax him to sing for me again, I played my flute. When that didn't work, I whistled and spoke to him in a lulling voice.

Escape was his sole intention. The only time he stood perfectly still was whenever a cat slunk across the patio. Then Gilguerro's heart would pound.

Pierre and I discussed building a 4' x 5' cage in one corner of the study until it occurred to us that the more room Gilguerro had the more damage he might do to himself. When the sun began to set, I draped a scarf over the cage. What a relief to hear him finally stop thrashing.

"I hope he lives," Jennifer said when she saw him. She slept in the study that night to watch over him. In the morning she was happy to report that Gilguerro had spent the entire night peacefully with his head tucked under his wing.

I removed the scarf from the cage. Gilguerro sat quietly listening while I played my flute for him but when I attempted to refill his water and seed dish he began to beat his wings frantically against the bars. It worried me that he might prevent any future chance of taking flight by hurting himself. It felt more and more ludicrous to keep him in a cage when obviously he had sung to me in hopes of escape.

I filled the birdfeeder that hung from the tree outside my study with sesame seeds, and carried Gilguerro's cage outside. I held it up towards the tree, unlatched and swung open the little door. My hope was that he would notice the feeder full with seed and decide on that tree as a fine place to live. I wanted him to stay and sing. I wanted to watch him in his freedom.

Gilguerro didn't move. I reached in and wrapped my fingers around him, gently pressing his little wings close to his body as I lifted him out of the cage into the open air.

His eyes were frantically blinking when I set him on the tree limb right beside the feeder but he made no attempt to fly off.

For several minutes he sat perfectly still keeping his eyes fixed on me. Then he seemed to be checking out the landscape. Finally he realized that he was actually free. That very second, he spread his wings, lifted up off the branch and flew to the crimson bougainvillea vine growing beside my study. He cocked his head and looked back at me. What a joy to see him fly!

His tiny lustrous eyes shone excitedly as he turned his head from side to side and saw only sky and trees. I've heard that when blind people regain their sight the world is frightening, no longer tangible in a tactile sense. Suddenly they are confronted with the dimension of depth never before experienced.

The world must have seemed alarmingly vast to Gilguerro at first. I began to wonder if possibly he had been captured as a fledgling and had grown up in a cage.

"Don't fly towards the street!" I shouted at him when he turned to gaze in that direction.

Much to my relief he flew toward Margaret's garden. With great gusto, he sailed towards her house until he hit her glass door with a thud.

Could I reach Gilguerro before her cat did?

I raced down the stairs into her garden and across her patio where Gilguerro was staggering around.

Just as I bent to scoop him up, he jumped into the air and madly flapped his wings until they lifted him up. He soared off to a lower limb of the big cypress tree in the center of the garden, restoring my confidence in his ability to cope with his newfound freedom.

He paused to recover while he glanced around at the endless space available to him. Then he flew to a distant jacaranda tree. Even though it thrilled me to see him fly free, at the same time I felt an incredible loss knowing that I might never see him again or hear his sweet song. I wanted to believe that he would return to the tree in front of my study to eat from the feeder, but I didn't think it too likely.

All afternoon, to no avail, I watched and listened for Gilguerro's return. Jennifer quickly put things into perspective when I told her how sad I felt that he was gone.

"What if you were stuck in jail because some people thought you were special," she said. "And what if, yes, they made it a little nicer than the jail you were in before. Would you rather be in the bigger, nicer jail or set free?"

I watched and listened for Gilguerro, but after several weeks passed, I began to wonder if I would even recognize his song if I heard it. Because I began listening for him very carefully I heard the jay crabbing in a nearby tree, the kiss-ka-dee repeating his name, and one day I heard a very cheerful song that led me to discovering a red house finch perched on top of the cypress tree. When the house finch began appearing every day, I wondered how long I had been oblivious to his presence in our garden. It amazed me that I had been unaware for so long of the songs that were being sung all around me. I wondered how many other worlds I was missing.

I kept the feeder full in hopes that Gilguerro would return. I never saw him again. But once, maybe because I wanted so badly to hear him, I thought I heard his song. I had given him freedom and in exchange he had ushered me into a world full of birdsong.

Before long, the red house finch claimed the feeder as his own and became the songbird flying free in our garden.

CHAPTER 12

The Red Bird

Without fail the red bird sang every day, often for hours at a time from on top of the tall cypress tree. Like a Christmas star, the red bird would glow in the sun as he sang his cheerful song.

Sometimes he reminded me of an enthusiastic gossip at a cocktail party; the person who takes great pleasure in being the first to tell the news. Instead of a melodic warble like Gilguerro's, the red bird's song was more like chatter.

Whenever I was in a bad mood or upset about something, his cheerfulness either reminded me to look at the bright side or infuriated me because he could consistently sing his happy song as if there were no people going hungry in Mexico, as if there were no troubles at all in the world. Often I found myself wishing that my stories would flow as easily as his songs.

Several months after I began putting seed in the feeder for the red bird, I was in the study when he flew down with his two daughters to land on the steps right outside the screen door. It was a thrill to see them up close. I liked thinking that he was showing them off to me, and it felt good that he trusted me enough to lead his fledglings to my study porch. Every now and then they would return while I sat very quietly in the study to watch them hop around in search of seed.

One day, when I came to the study, I found one of the red bird's daughters dead on the step, the obvious work of some cat. Surely the red bird was aware of what had happened and yet he was singing his song from the tip of the cypress, a song as cheerful as the one he had sung every other day.

My greatest fear in life had always been that something might happen to my daughters. I knew I couldn't bear that kind of pain.

The red bird's quick detachment from the loss of his fledgling amazed me. He kept coming to eat from the feeder but never again did he lead his fledglings to my study porch.

CHAPTER 13

Jennifer's Love of Animals

I never managed to figure out a way that Jennifer could have an animal that wouldn't set off Carla's allergies.

At the end of the school year, Jennifer asked if she could bring Fred, the white rat who was her classroom's mascot, home for the summer. I tried to talk her out of it by reminding her of our plans to spend a month in California. I only had two months off from teaching school; summer was precious.

But when she found someone to take care of Fred during our vacation, I agreed. Jennifer has always known what she wants and how to get it. Fred stayed in his cage on the front porch. Much to my surprise, after I got used to the fact that he was a rat, I took quite a liking to him. He adored Jenny. Often I would look out the window and see Jennifer running around in Riverside Park with Fred traipsing after her.

Whenever I came home after a late night out, Fred would leap out of a deep sleep to greet me. I started feeding him Ritz crackers with cheese and bits of avocado. I think he preferred living with us over being manhandled by thirty children at the school.

In the fall, when school started again, Jennifer couldn't manage the cage on the bus by herself so I told her I would deliver Fred to the school by car. But each day when I went to take him, I couldn't bring myself to give him up.

At the end of the second week of school, Jennifer came home and announced that her teacher and the other students were getting upset.

"They don't think you're ever going to return him," she said with complete understanding of why I had been stalling. "You have to bring Fred back, Mom."

So I did.

A month later Fred died from a cancerous tumor and Jennifer was heartbroken.

The next creature put in Jennifer's care was a neighbor's bird. When Martha went camping for a long weekend with her family, she gave Jenny the key to their house and instructions on what to feed her canary.

On the morning they were to return, a strange storm woke me up well before dawn. There was an eerie light in the sky and a spooky silence filled the air like it does right before the roar of an oncoming tornado.

Jennifer and I walked over to feed the bird. Before I even got near the cage, Jennifer was screaming, "Ohhhhhh noooo!"

The little yellow bird was lying on the floor of his cage. "Look," I said, "he's going to get up. He's just resting." I couldn't believe that I was saying such a thing when the canary was obviously dead.

Did I think the bird would somehow revive himself just

because I wanted it so badly for Jennifer?

"I killed it. I killed it. Oh, they'll be so mad at me."

"No they won't. It wasn't anything you did. Maybe the bird was terrified of the storm. They can die from fright. That happens you know."

Nothing I said convinced her that it wasn't her fault. We buried the bird in Martha's garden and Jennifer found some wildflowers growing at the edge of the park to put on the grave. It reminded me of the many bird funerals I had held under the weeping willow tree. Only this time it never occurred to either of us to put the bird in a jar.

I went with Jennifer to tell Martha how she had discovered the dead bird. "Oh I'm so sorry, Jenny. You know the day we left on vacation, the kids let Wolfgang out of the cage and chased him all over the living room. By the time I put him back inside, he was frantic. Maybe that's why he died." Jenny brought Martha to the garden to show her Wolgang's lovely grave.

* * *

By the time we moved to Mexico, Carla had outgrown her allergies and had agreed that it was a good idea to get Jenny a big protective dog. New to the country, I believed the U.S. propaganda about how dangerous it is to live in Mexico. I hadn't yet discovered that almost all Latin Americans consider children as blessings from God. Even if it is a struggle to feed them, children are never seen as burdens. I thought a guard dog was necessary, because we hadn't yet experienced the love and protection the Mexican townspeople continuously expressed towards both of my daughters.

Once we saw the half-starved and cowering street dogs, with their skin stretched taut over their bones, we knew we would have to worry about disease if we just took in a stray. Jennifer quickly solved the problem by deciding on one of the curly-haired toy poodle puppies that the neighbors had bred to sell. Their dog had papers and so did the dog who had fathered the pups, making the litter quite valuable.

The toy poodle she chose was definitely not the protector I had in mind, but when I saw his darling little face, shiny coal black eyes and crooked mouth that made him look like he was smiling, I understood why Jennifer adored him.

Whenever she went down to the square in the middle of town, she brought Poquito with her, usually carrying him in her arms like a baby. Even though Jennifer made him a lovely little bed out of a cardboard box lined with a handmade doll-quilt, Poquito only took afternoon naps in it. At night he slept on the edge of her bed.

Pierre and I decided to allow him to sleep there because moving to Mexico was a difficult adjustment for Jennifer to make, and she hadn't found any friends yet. It didn't help that Carla already had a boyfriend and from him was learning Spanish very quickly.

Poquito would bark as ferociously as he could muster when I entered Jenny's room at night to check on her. "Oh, Poquito," I would say gently.

He always recognized my voice and stopped barking immediately. "Are you protecting my angel?" He would wag his tail full speed.

Poquito loved to slide on his belly across the tiled floor. Over and over again he would come sailing from the kitchen to glide the length of the dining room floor while we ate.

As he grew bigger, he began chewing holes in the rattan rugs. "We're living in a rented house," I kept reminding Jenny. Then I would repeat Pierre's constant complaint, "You've got to train him." Soon Poquito was leaving a good-sized turd in my study almost every day.

"You've got to train Poquito."

"I am," she would say in earnest.

One night after Jennifer demanded that Pierre and I sit down in the living room, she had Poquito show us all his tricks. He could shake hands and lick her face. He could stand on his hind legs and turn around. As she was running him through a whole series of circus-like tricks, we realized that neither of us had explained to Jenny what "training" meant.

We all doted on Poquito. Then one day he disappeared. Jennifer and I frantically searched the house and garden for him without any luck. Then we walked down the cobblestone hill calling his name. At the bottom of the street stood a traffic cop who said he hadn't seen Poquito. We put a plea out over the radio and made signs that we hung up all over town, but never again did we see or hear anything about Poquito.

We assumed he had been kidnapped.

* * *

Soon after, the house we were renting was sold. Even before we moved, I knew Jennifer was plotting to find another animal to bring home.

CHAPTER 14

Two Chickens from the Market

Jennifer came home one afternoon with a little paper bag in her hand. I recognized the slashes at the top as air holes. She emptied the contents onto the kitchen floor. Two tiny chickens no more than a day old, stumbled around barely able to see, chirping constantly for their mother. I doubt whether Jennifer had even given a thought as to where we would put them when they grew up.

Maybe because I had brought Gilguerro home and had considered buying the ravens, Jennifer thought it would be a good idea to bring a couple of feathered creatures home from the market. I wasn't about to discourage her until Pierre took me aside and explained that the chickens had been taken away from their mother much too soon and probably wouldn't live long.

I tried to explain this to Jennifer but instead of listening she busied herself with setting the chickens in a cardboard box along with a jar lid of water and one with grain. Then she put the box in the middle of the living room floor.

When I came home to make supper late that afternoon, Jennifer was nowhere in sight, but the chickens, who had fallen into their water dish, were shivering. Their cotton-like fluff was all matted down so you could see their pimply grey-blue skin. One of them was lying on his side obviously close to death.

"Pierre!" I shouted, becoming extremely upset at the obviously imminent death of these chicks.

"Well, don't just stand there," Pierre said as he picked up the chick in the most trouble and held it an inch from his lips. He began blowing gently on the bird until its down fluffed up and the tiny creature began chirping again. I did the same to the other chick, but even while I was blowing warm air on the bird, I didn't believe for a minute that we could revive these scrawny little creatures.

Pierre brought in his desk lamp and set it beside the box. The chickens snuggled close together under this source of heat and slept. When Jennifer arrived home and heard about the close call, she spent the night on the couch right beside her chickens. Around midnight one of the chicks died and Jennifer surprised us by taking it quite calmly. It wasn't even dawn, however, when I heard Jenny calling, "Maaaaaaaa," as she raced up the stairs toward our bedroom. I knew by the tone of her voice that the other chicken had just died. She wasn't consoled when Pierre repeated what he had told me earlier about how the birds didn't have much of a chance, because they were taken away from their mother too soon.

Together Jennifer and I dug a hole in the grass patch and buried the chicks side by side.

It seemed somewhat uncanny to me that while I was writing about bird burials in my novel, the red bird's daughter, the two chickens and a mourning dove who hit our bedroom window had all been buried in the grass patch. Synchronicity seemed to be happening more and more often but I didn't like the fact that the connection seemed to be with death.

It was right about this time that Pierre and I went off to our friend's cottage and were nearly asphyxiated. I wondered if having been saved by Bird in my dream was a sign that our luck had turned.

As a young child, I had sensed that the birds in the trees observed my funerals. When I thought about this and took a look around my garden in San Miguel, I began to notice birds that I had never seen or heard before. Had they been watching the recent burials in the grass patch? I concluded that they had when one afternoon, I looked up and saw seven mourning doves sitting side by side on a branch in the peppercorn tree. The grey of their feathers was the same exact color as the bark. The birds cooed while they preened one another with great care and tenderness.

CHAPTER 15

Hummer

One morning, I hiked around town doing errands. I stopped at the bank, the bakery, the post office, and shopped at the market. Finally, I climbed the cobblestone hill, anxious to get home. When I arrived, I found Pierre on the upstairs patio. At the precise moment I handed him the mail, a bird hit our bedroom window with a thud.

Oh no, I can't bury a bird today, I muttered to myself as I dashed down the spiral stairs with Pierre close behind me. I won't accept that reality.

But my cynical side leapt at the opportunity to remind me that I had no control over such things.

When I reached the garden, my eyes frantically searched the area below the window until I caught sight of a single feather lying on the grass. "Oh good," I said to Pierre while bending over to pick it up. "The bird must have flown off."

As I bent closer to the ground, however, I saw that it wasn't a feather at all. It was a tiny hummingbird lying on the grass. His eyes were closed, and his long thin tongue, like the pistil of a flower, was hanging out beyond his long narrow beak. I assumed he was dead until I saw his heart pounding. While I watched, his heart visibly began to slow down.

Because of the novella I was writing, where I made Gloria a hummingbird expert, I had been doing some research. All the information I had recently gathered quickly came to mind. Except at night when the hummingbird slows way down, like a bear in hibernation, its metabolism is faster than any other living creature; therefore, it must eat every fifteen seconds.

Remembering this, I ran into the kitchen while Pierre held the hummingbird in the palm of his hand. I grabbed a jar lid and hastily mixed together some sugar and water.

We laid the bird's tongue and beak in the jar lid. His eyes blinked open. He sucked his tongue back into his beak. On the second sip, the hummer's wings flashed open and stayed open; but he remained sitting in Pierre's hand perfectly still.

In the sunlight the delicate lacework of his wings reminded me of the intricacy of a spider web. How often does one get to see a hummingbird's wings up close? It was a gift to be able to see this incredible sight. It reminded me of the first time I noticed the magnificence of a snowflake.

His green iridescent body sparkled like a jewel. After taking a third sip, the bird shot out into the air with the same startling quickness with which he had opened his eyes and wings.

The thrill of this experience made me think about the joy doctors must feel when they save a patient.

Instead of the burial I had expected, we witnessed the hummingbird take flight. Throughout the afternoon I felt grateful for my connection to birds. I also felt thankful for my father who feeds hummingbirds, for Pierre, who taught me to assume that lives can be saved, and for synchronicity itself. I felt blessed by the hummingbird who lived.

* * *

The very next day after the hummingbird hit the window, I noticed him sucking nectar from the orange trumpet flowers that grew from the vine-covered wall adjacent to our bedroom window. Because he returned every day to spend several hours in our garden, I began to take his presence for granted. Whenever I sat by the window writing, he would dart over and hover in mid-air a few inches from my face on the other side of the glass. He would take a good look at me, as if he was checking things out. I began talking to him whenever he appeared.

"Hi, Hummer," I'd say. Sometimes, while he was feeding at the flowers, I would call to him and he would back up in mid-air, pulling his long narrow beak from the center of the flower and dash over to scrutinize me.

Once, as I was sitting on the upstairs balcony, Hummer flew quite close and did a few aerial nose-dives and fancy twists. At first I thought I was only imagining that Hummer was performing for my delight. After several minutes of the most amazing display, Hummer returned to the vine flowers.

I called to Pierre to tell him what had just taken place. Of course he was skeptical. He didn't believe that Hummer had actually performed for me.

When I saw the ‘oh sure’ expression on his face, I felt challenged. "Hummer? Hi, Hummer. Come dance for me," I called feeling a bit ridiculous. I must admit that I was as amazed as Pierre was when Hummer actually darted over to us and repeated his aerial tricks. I suppose it could have been pure chance. But soon I was given reason to believe that Hummer could tune in to me.

Time and time again, whenever I was upset about something, Hummer would appear. It was as if he picked up on my unhappiness. He would fly over to the window and hover there, checking in on me.

Hummer was not only a constant source of delight, but also a reminder to believe in miracles. I felt as if I was partaking in something wondrous whenever Hummer would fly right up to me and hover just a few inches from my face. He was also a source of inspiration for my novel, yet I knew that I was still lacking some essential experience I needed in order to write a believable story about how a woman's relationship with birds changes her.

In the novel, I had given Bird too many human qualities. Somehow my fiction didn't resonate with the essential truth I was searching for. I knew that because something crucial was missing within me, I couldn't relay it in my book.

CHAPTER 16

Big Lunker and Little Guy

I didn't love him any less because he was a duck. Lunker entered my life quite unexpectedly, and our bonding took place before I even realized what was happening.

It all began one afternoon when I walked into Jennifer's room and noticed a big lump moving under her quilt. "What's that?" I asked pointing towards the bed.

Jennifer shrugged her shoulders.

"What do you mean you don't know? It's moving. I can see it. Jenny, what kind of creature did you bring home this time?"

She flung back the quilt and gathered something up so quickly that I only caught a glimpse of yellow before she rushed up saying, "Now shut your eyes and hold out your hands."

Even though I wasn't in the mood for games, I couldn't refuse her. Soon I felt a fuzzy creature in each palm. Upon opening my eyes, I could hardly believe that the tiny yellow ducks, each with a cotton ball puff on top of his head and a little carrot colored beak, were real. I promptly agreed that the two Peking ducklings were adorable, but I told Jenny that if she were allowed to keep them, she would have to clean up after the ducks, feed them, and find a cage.

We approached Pierre on the subject. He set down his newspaper and shook his head. "They'll grow fast. They'll be big and white and ugly in no time. I hope you both realize that you'll be constantly cleaning up after them."

The ducks spent most of their days sitting on the grass patch next to the white irises or under the shade of a two-foot tall poplar seedling. Together they would waddle over to their food dish and every now and then over to the rose bush to dig for bugs. Very quickly they had become inseparable.

Before practicing my flute, I would bring the ducks into the house and set them in a big cardboard box beside my feet. The smallest duck usually nestled in the corner and slept, but the other duck always stood erect and peeked over the top of the box. With his head turned to one side, he would gaze at me with his little black shiny eye. For however long I played, he listened without distraction.

I thrived on such attention because usually whenever I practiced, Jennifer and Carla would leave the house, and Pierre would run a bath or turn on the television to out-noise me. I didn't blame them; my tone was often shrill. But the big duck seemed to love my music. This one grew fast. We named him Big Lunker. His fuzz soon became pure white feathers. He walked with his head held high. When his topknot became an elegant swirl that looked like a pompadour, he was the prince of birds, a true aristocrat.

The other duck remained quite small, as if he were the runt of the litter. We called him Little Guy. He continued to keep a tinge of yellow even when his white feathers had finally formed. Little Guy didn't have Lunker's intelligent curiosity, but he was good-natured, and he adored Lunker.

Every morning at dawn the ducks would crawl out of the big cage that Jennifer had borrowed from a friend and set beside the garage where the firewood was stored. Promptly at 8:00, the ducks would waddle over to the grass patch to sit beside their food dish and wait for me to bring them their breakfast of lettuce, celery, and groats. I never complained about being the one who fed them because Jennifer was always rushing off to school or busy with her homework and friends. I rather enjoyed the fact that the ducks were vegetarians who ate the trimmings from our salads.

It was much more pleasant to prepare their breakfast than boiling up chicken livers each morning as I used to do for our cat.

I did, however, grumble about being the only one who hosed down the patio.

One morning upon waking up late, I realized how strangely quiet it was in the garden. I hadn't heard a sound from the ducks. Usually when I was even ten minutes late with their breakfast, they would be squawking. I went outside and looked all around but didn't see them anywhere. I could tell that they hadn't been on the patio. I rushed over to the cage and saw that Little Guy was so weak he could hardly hold his head up. Lunker sat silently beside him. I reached into the cage to lift Little Guy out, but Lunker raised such a fuss I had to set Little Guy right back inside. I walked away feeling helpless. Lunker obviously wanted privacy. He needed to cope with Little Guy's illness by himself.

Every half hour I returned to check on the ducks, and each time I looked into the cage, Little Guy's head drooped a bit more. Lunker remained perfectly still and silent beside him. Around noon when I checked on them again, there was no sign of Little Guy. Lunker looked huge; he seemed to fill the entire cage. I soon discovered that he was sitting on top of Little Guy either to warm him after he had died or to help him along at the end by smothering him.

At first, I debated whether or not I should wait for Jennifer to come home from school before I buried Little Guy but decided I would spare her this funeral. As I squatted on the ground to dig a hole beside the poplar seedling, I tried to keep my back towards Lunker, but he waddled over to sit right beside me. He watched me bury his friend.

After I planted some marigolds on the grave, Lunker returned to the cage and climbed back inside. Several times that day I tried to coax him out by enticing him with food but he always turned his head away. That evening, I stood beside the cage and played my flute for him.

He never once even glanced out at me. The next day, when he still refused to leave the cage, I presented him with a plate of sardines, his favorite food. Again he turned his head away. This worried me.

Late that afternoon, I took him out of the cage and set him in the grass patch thinking he would soon become distracted and begin to dig for bugs, but he immediately waddled over to the cage and climbed inside. I took him out again, and this time I shut the door behind him making it impossible for him to get back in. He headed right for the garage wall and sat facing it. No one could cheer him up, not even Jennifer who tried with hilarious antics.

On the third day I couldn't bear it any longer. He hadn't eaten a thing since Little Guy died, nor had he once bothered to preen himself. That was unusual for Lunker, who always took great pride in keeping himself pristinely clean. Never before had I seen even a speck of dust on his snow white feathers.

I just had to do something to console him. But what? I pulled up a lawn chair, picked up Lunker and sat down in the chair holding him in my arms. I ran my hand down his back over and over again stroking his velvety feathers. Soon he snuggled up against my breast, hung his head over my shoulder and tucked his beak into the hair at the nape of my neck.

I held him close and petted him, while whispering in his ear, "It's all right, Lunker. It's all right. Nancy loves you."

After a while, I heard the strangest noise. It sounded like a puppy whining. At first I didn't realize the crying was coming from Lunker. We stayed in the lawn chair for nearly two hours. While he grieved, I stroked his feathers and told him how much I loved him. I didn't realize that we had bonded; I now had become the focus of Lunker's undivided love and attention.

CHAPTER 17

Lunky Love

After I had held Lunker in my arms, he was finally willing to eat. In fact he eagerly slurped up the lentil soup and gulped down a whole can of sardines.

He didn't stay in the cage anymore except to sleep at night. I'm not sure who loved it most when I scooped him up into my arms to stroke him.

Every once in a while when I held him, Lunker would imitate his grieving sounds; it became his way of getting me to ruffle his feathers while I called him my "Lunky, love."

Whenever I worked in the garden, Lunker followed me around like an obedient dog. While I practiced my flute outside on the patio, Lunker would stand beside me, captivated. Once, when I sat with him on the grass patch imitating his duck sounds, “babop, babop, babop,” he joined in. This is how our duet first began.

Lunker couldn't bear it when I was in the house. I'd glance out a window and see him on the other side of the glass staring in at me. Jennifer didn't seem to mind that Lunker had become so attached to me; she was involved with her first boyfriend and had lost all interest in ducks.

I began turning down social invitations because I wanted to spend more time with Lunker. At first, I invented excuses, but eventually didn't bother trying to explain. It took a while, but Pierre got used to visiting people without me.

* * *

One hot day, when Lunker and I were home alone and had grown weary of singing duets, I carried him into the bathroom. After putting the plug into the tub, I filled it to the brim. Lunker dove in, swam underwater to one end of the tub, made an aquatic turn, and zipped to the opposite end. This, he repeated at an incredible speed. Sometimes he would surge up, pop his head out and skim the water while flapping his wings. I had great fun sitting on the vanity, laughing, while Lunker performed his tricks.

As I was carrying him outside to set him on the grass in the sun so he could preen, Lunker cocked his head to one side and looked at me intently, just as he did whenever I played my flute. What was he thinking? Before I could even guess, he swung his head around to face me, pressed his bill against my lips and kissed me.

The thrill of that kiss actually made me feel weak in the knees. He may have bonded to me on the day in the garden when I had consoled him; but it was when his bill touched my lips that I bonded to him.

I felt the strongest urge to declare my love for Lunker to the whole world, but I knew it would be impossible to explain how I had fallen head over heels in love with a duck.

One sunny day, Lunker and I were having a particularly pleasant time together seated on the grass beside the rose bush. I improvised a song, which Lunker mimicked with gusto, and then I laughed at the cleverness of our duet and ruffled his neck feathers in the manner that he loved. He seemed ultra excited that day by my voice and touch. Soon his whole body began to vibrate. At the time, I didn't think it strange that I should be feeling an intense affection for Lunker, nor did I question the possibility of it being mutual.

I was caught up in pure sensation of the most delightful kind, and Lunker appeared to be experiencing the same. We continued to sing while his entire body shook. Each individual feather seemed to whirr.

I soon realized that Lunker's fixation on me wasn't fair to him. He needed a duck to love.

I decided it would actually be easier to keep the patio clean if we had two ducks. Lunker wouldn't be following me all around or peeking in the windows; he would spend much more time on the grass sitting with his new partner.

The very next day, Jennifer stopped at the market but she was told that it wasn't the season for ducks. It might be quite some time before they received any, and it was highly unlikely that they would ever have another Peking.

I called several friends, asking them to help spread the word around town that I needed a mate for Lunker. I also put an ad in the local gringo newspaper.

A week later, a woman called to say that she had a duck. When I explained how my beautiful Peking needed a mate, she said hers was just the duck I was looking for.

Thrilled, I gave her my address and asked her to bring her duck over. When the doorbell rang, Lunker waddled right beside me as I went to greet them. Preening his pure white feathers and fluffing himself up for the visitors, he was impressively handsome. In comparison to the woman's ill-fed flea-ridden duck, Lunker looked like a snow prince.

The woman set her duck down beside Lunker so they could become acquainted. Apparently she had misunderstood what I told her on the telephone, because she announced that her duck would make the perfect husband.

The scruffy grey-feathered visitor was intrigued by the majestic bird with the pompadour puff, but Lunker kept trying to escape the creature who pursued him.

I quickly explained that the match would never work because my duck was also a male.

"No, it's not," the woman insisted, as she grabbed Lunker by the legs, held him upside down in the air and peered at his underside. "Uh-huh, this is a female alright."

Lunker was incensed. His eyes smoldered. No one had ever treated him with such utter disrespect. I felt equally offended and didn't hesitate to usher the woman to the door, exclaiming that Lunker was indeed a male.

Without a moment's hesitation, Lunker waddled over to his cage and climbed inside. He felt totally violated.

CHAPTER 18

Finding a Wife for Lunker

Jennifer and I returned to the market several times without any luck. Then one day, I had the notion that if we visualized the perfect mate for Lunker she would somehow appear.

Not wanting to dispute my belief in the power of positive thinking, Jennifer sat with me in the garden with her eyes closed. In silence we created an image in our minds: a princess of a duck, a creature to capture Lunker's heart.

After meditating in this way I turned towards Lunker and with complete confidence told him, "We're getting you a wife, and not a wife with fleas either. Soon you'll have a duck of your own to love, Lunky. Yes you will. Just you wait."

To our astonishment, Lunker immediately began preening. He kept fluffing up his feathers as though he knew exactly what we were talking about. He couldn't make himself gorgeous enough.

Late that afternoon, while I was cooking supper, I glanced out the kitchen window to see a mourning dove fly down and land on the grass three feet from where Lunker was sitting. Soon, another dove arrived and then another until there were seven mourning doves scooting around exploring Lunker's yard.

Lunker, who by now looked breathtakingly handsome, sat and watched the doves eat from his dish. He seemed a bit startled, but I could see their presence intrigued him. For a long time he sat perfectly still and observed the doves as they scooted through the grass, dipping down for seeds and then scurrying over to sip from his water dish.

Though the doves seemed to ignore him, Lunker looked quite pleased at the mere proximity of other birds. Suddenly he stood up. Before he could take a single step toward them, whirrrr whooooosh one dove flew off and the others immediately followed. In an instant they were gone.

Lunker looked puzzled. Then he became sad and went to sit under the poplar seedling. But within minutes, whirrrr, whirrrr all the doves returned.

Pretending not to notice them, Lunker kept his back toward the doves and preened a bit more while he watched them over his shoulder. He had learned not to make any sudden moves.

During the days that followed, the seven mourning doves flew down often. They helped occupy his time. I had the distinct impression that Lunker believed Jennifer and I were responsible for their initial arrival. Was he pleased or disappointed? Perhaps he felt we had summoned the wrong kind of bird. I tried to make it up to him by holding and petting him more often.

Just as I was once again feeling comfortable being the sole object of Lunker's affection, Jennifer arrived home with a baby duck. In comparison, Lunker looked huge. This was an ordinary farm duck with a shy disposition. She wasn't a Peking. It was stupid, I guess, but we thought we could just hand over a little duck to Lunker and he would care for her and love her until she grew big enough for their courtship to begin. At that time, I had yet to experience the violent side of Lunker's nature.

CHAPTER 19

Becky

With the little duck named Becky in my hand, I went to sit on the grass beside Lunker to make the introductions. I was certain he'd be thrilled.

I set Becky in my lap and draped my arm around Lunker. I ran my hand up and down his neck -- an action that he always loved. But this time his body didn't begin to vibrate.

Before I knew what was happening, Lunker reached down and grabbed one of Becky's tiny legs with his beak. He was trying to rip it off. Without even thinking, I closed my hand tight around his neck to let him know that if he did Becky any harm I would snap the life out of him.

At that precise moment, time stopped. Lunker gazed at me in disbelief while I glared back in total determination. We were all three hideously connected.

Lunker opened his beak and released Becky's leg. I let go of his neck. The thought of having come that close to killing Lunker with my bare hands sickened me. As for Lunker, I think he felt not only betrayed but totally rejected. I could see in his eyes that our bond had been broken.

Because Lunker wanted to kill Becky the first chance he got, I kept her inside the house until she grew to maturity. My consolation was the belief that, as soon as Becky was big enough to be safe in the garden, Lunker would take a romantic interest in her.

Sometimes I worried, because Becky was growing so slowly even though she seemed healthy enough. Now Becky sat beside me while I practiced my flute in the house. But it wasn't the same. She either dozed off or grew bored and began strolling around to explore her environment.

When Lunker heard me playing music and knew that another duck was in the house with me, he would come stand outside the window and stare in with an almost maniacal look.

I would stop playing sometimes and say to Becky, "He's upset now, but soon you'll grow up and he'll discover what a wonderful duck you are."

* * *

Our elderly landlady Margaret arrived unannounced one day to check up on things. She saw Becky scoot across the living room floor.

"What's that, a chicken? You can't have a chicken in my house."

I tried to explain the situation. She wouldn't listen. Quickly, she made it clear that we would be evicted if I didn't get rid of both ducks fast. It didn't seem to matter to her that we had lived there for two years and spent a lot of time fixing up the house and creating a flower garden.

I knew perfectly well that there were no other houses to rent as lovely as Margaret's and I couldn't make Jennifer, Carla and Pierre move out of their home just so I could keep Lunker. I had no choice but to promise Margaret that as soon as the ducks became a couple, I would find them a new home. I tried to convince myself that Lunker might actually enjoy living on a ranch in the country, especially if he had a nice pond to swim in. But would he survive such a drastic change after growing up so pampered and protected in my garden?

That very afternoon, as though in answer to my question, I read an article in Audubon Magazine: Even after living in domesticity, if returned to its natural habitat, a duck can quickly adapt. That was reassuring, but the next statement made me sick at heart: in a short time the duck may not recognize its former owner.

I suffered at the possibility that one day Lunker might not know me, and agonized over the thought of spending even one day without him. I couldn't imagine what my life would be like without Lunker. I figured the only way I could possibly give him up was if I found him paradise.

I began spending much more time with him. When he had me all to himself, he behaved as though no trouble had ever passed between us. But as soon as I went into the house, Lunker would become frantic. It was as though he immediately forgot that I had just given him my undivided attention.

All that concerned him was that another duck was in the house with me.

CHAPTER 20

Lunker and Becky

When Becky grew to be about half Lunker's size, I put her out in the garden leaving her there a bit longer each day. In case he still entertained any malicious ideas, I stayed nearby. But to my surprise, Lunker never again made an aggressive move towards Becky. I think it pleased him that she was finally out of the house during the day. (We brought her back inside to sleep at night.) Now that she had grown bigger, he never let her out of his sight in the garden.

It was a relief to be able to leave them alone for long periods of time. Soon the ducks were spending the entire day together. Wherever Becky went, Lunker would follow. After growing up in the house, Becky had a lot of exploring to do in the garden. Back and forth they waddled across the patio making it necessary for me to hose it down at least five times a day. Although their relationship had developed according to plan, to my surprise sometimes I felt rejected, especially when I would go out to the garden to play my flute, and Lunker would ignore me.

A short while after they began spending their days together, Jennifer's friend came to get the cage he had lent us. That was all right; Lunker no longer needed it. He could scare off the neighborhood cats. Because there was a high wall enclosing our garden and patio, no dogs had ever come sniffing around.

We felt absolutely certain that Lunker would protect Becky. Jennifer and I agreed the time was ripe for Becky to become Lunker's wife. Jenny placed a large cardboard box on its side and hung a scarf over the opening so the ducks could have their privacy, yet come and go quite easily. Then she served them their wedding food. Greedily they slurped down a big portion of sardines soaked in tomato sauce.

Just before dark, I went out to make sure that Becky felt alright about spending her first night with Lunker. I noticed that Lunker, who was always meticulous about his appearance, had orange streaks that looked like war paint under his eyes reaching up towards his pompadour. The tomato sauce from the sardines had streaked his feathers and made him look strangely primitive. It was as if he had painted himself for the wedding ritual. The way Lunker was prancing around and preening, we could see how excited he was.

I coaxed Becky into Lunker's box. He followed eagerly.

* * *

Thinking I would read for a while, I tucked myself into bed but nothing held my interest. Instead I put the books aside and began reminiscing about how it had been with Lunker before Becky's arrival. I soon grew curious about what was going on between the ducks. Telling myself I just wanted to let in the cool evening breeze, I opened the bedroom window to listen.

All was quiet except for an occasional bus grinding up a distant hill and the barking of a street dog. I returned to bed and slipped into a deep relaxed sleep, only to be startled awake by a loud frantic squawking. Knowing that it had come from Becky, I leapt out of bed and raced into the garden.

In the moonlight, Becky was walking around in circles on the patio, looking extremely agitated, while Lunker – still wearing his war paint – poked his head out of the box to watch her.

I found another cardboard box in the garage and set it beside Lunker's. Becky stepped inside. Lunker followed. She dashed out to climb into the other box. He followed her again. This continued until Lunker finally got the message, and gave up his pursuit. For the next two nights they slept separately. But at dawn on the third day, I looked into Lunker's box and saw them huddled together. From then on Becky seemed content being a female duck.

Lunker considered Becky his sole property and wouldn't allow anyone to come close to her. In fact, if anyone approached her, he would go after them rather viciously.

If I went out to water the rose bush, Lunker would nip at my ankles. He didn't want me anywhere near the grass patch. When I was cutting some chives, he snuck up behind me. He pinched my leg so hard he created a fat purple welt. After that, whenever I saw him sneaking up behind me, I would kick at him, but within seconds he would return to pinch me again.

I filled a bucket of water and during one of his attacks, dumped it over his head. He thought that was a great game. At first I had difficulty believing that Lunker would intentionally try to hurt me. I guess he feared that given the chance to get near Becky I might take her back into the house. Whatever the impetus, I didn't much like the fact that our relationship was disintegrating, nor did I delight in the increasing number of welts he inflicted on me.

I'd push him away; I'd kick at him as hard as I dared. But he would eventually manage to give me yet another nasty pinch.

Pierre asked me why I put up with it. "Why don't you just teach him a quick lesson? Really haul off and let him have it." But I couldn't bear to hurt Lunker, even though he obviously had no difficulty hurting me.

Once I put a box over his head and watched him blindly walk around in circles. Even that punishment made me feel bad. Pierre kept reminding me of my promise to the landlady. But I always panicked at the thought of giving up Lunker. I stalled for time by insisting that Becky was still a bit too young to adjust to a new environment.

This plot worked until Pierre discovered that a writer named Warren Schultz lived on a gorgeous ranch beside a shallow river five miles outside of San Miguel, and he had two Peking ducks of his own.

CHAPTER 21

Visiting Paradise

Before Pierre, Jennifer, and I climbed into the car, I packed a picnic lunch and fed sardines to the ducks. Even though Jennifer hadn't spent much time with Lunker lately, I could tell she felt sad, as she sat in the back seat beside the cardboard box that held Lunker. While Pierre drove, I held Becky in my lap on an old towel. I couldn't understand why I wasn't feeling more upset. Perhaps I didn't quite believe that we would really leave our ducks at Warren's house and drive off without them. Or was I finally fed up with Lunker's nasty pinching? Even though he was close enough to attack Jennifer, he never once tried it. He thought it was great fun to ride in the car. He liked to stare out the window and watch the trees whizz by.

We drove up a tree-lined dirt road past a vast cornfield to a tall stone fence that circled the property surrounding Warren's house and pond. As luck would have it, when we rang the bell at the iron gate, no one answered. Warren didn't have a telephone; he apparently treasured his privacy.

"We can have a picnic somewhere downstream," Pierre said after suggesting we hike beyond the meadow to walk along the river and introduce the ducks to the wild. Splashing and swimming in the water was Lunker's idea of fun. But the strong current and vastness of it all frightened Becky. She looked terribly vulnerable and small with her feathers all matted.

While we ate our lunch, I glanced over to the riverbank and saw Becky shivering as she stood under a pine seedling.

I jumped up, spilling the thermos of lemonade, and rushed off to rescue her, shouting over my shoulder that we had to leave for home right away. Jennifer dashed down to the river and snatched Lunker out of the water. She tucked him under her arm not at all concerned that he was soaking wet.

Pierre packed up what was left of our picnic and offered his shirt to use as a towel for Becky. He insisted we check back at Warren's before we left.

But I said no. Poor Becky needed to get home. It would be awful if she died on us now. I assured him that I would be willing to try again next week.

After taking a good look at her, Pierre couldn't help but agree. Jennifer gave a cheer. With a smile on her face and her arm around Lunker, she sang all the way home.

With Pierre's shirt, I rubbed Becky's feathers briskly, trying to dry her off and warm her at the same time. Fluffed up again and feeling safe in my lap, she finally stopped shivering.

Lunker had never once tried to attack me during the outing. I wondered if he had passed beyond his pinching phase. Except when he was swimming, he had followed right along beside me without incident.

By the time we arrived home, the sun was beginning to set. Back in familiar territory, Becky began to recuperate rapidly. Both ducks sat happily in the grass patch under a lovely pink and lilac-splashed sky, while I went into the house to fix them supper.

They eagerly slurped up the groats and lettuce. I sat beside Lunker with my arm draped around him and held Becky in my lap. Just as I was delighting in the turn of events that brought the ducks back home, Lunker lunged at me, grabbed my upper lip with his beak and yanked it with such force it felt as though he was ripping it off.

Without even thinking, I swung at him and knocked him over. He bounced right back up like one of those roly-poly dolls. With a smug look, he held his head aloof and peered at me with his little piercing black eye.

"I wish I had left you at the river to drown!" I shouted, as I raced into the house to get something to ease the pain of my throbbing, swollen lip.

Pierre must have seen what had happened; he was busily preparing an icepack.

"Now you'll be glad to get rid of him, won't you?"

I promptly agreed, but my anger had already begun to subside, as anger usually does if you vent it immediately. Only a part of me wanted to strike back at Lunker. Another part of me was merely hurt. Yet another part, the part even Lunker's nastiness never seemed to reach, was already despairing over the dreadful fact that, in one week, the ducks would be gone from my garden.

Holding the icepack against my throbbing lip, I lay down on the couch and tried to figure out what had prompted Lunker's vicious attack. Had he been aware of my intention to abandon him? Did he strike out to let me know just how betrayed he felt?

CHAPTER 22

All is Well

If surroundings reflect the person who lives there, I knew I didn't have a thing to be anxious about. Pink water lilies floated on the expansive pond beside Warren's blooming flower garden. Sensing my intense relationship to the ducks, Warren kindly reassured me that they would be in good hands.

Of course I knew that if I had searched the world over for duck paradise, I couldn't have found a better spot, but that didn't ease my grief. I felt as though I was abandoning the ducks, but managed to thank Pierre for finding them such a wonderful new home.

Had I not been a grown woman, I might have followed my impulse to fall to the ground, wrap my arms around Lunker and wail. I honestly wondered how I would be able to let him go.

After returning home, in the privacy of my room, I wept. An image of Lunker swimming gracefully through the pink lily pads consoled me.

* * *

The next weekend I went to see for myself if the ducks liked their new home. Both Pierre and Jennifer accompanied me. She brought along a tin of sardines. We lifted the latch on the front gate and stepped into the garden as Warren had told us to do whenever we came for a visit. I panicked at the thought that possibly *Audubon* had been right about how quickly a duck can forget its previous owner.

As we strolled down the green rolling hill towards the pond, I called out, "Lunker, oh Lunky love, Nancy's here to see you."

Suddenly, his head popped up out of the tall reeds along the shore, and he waddled up the hill singing, “babop, babop, babop.” I ran towards Lunker singing the same and scooped him up into my arms while Pierre opened the can of sardines. Jennifer dashed off to look for Becky and found her sitting quietly beside the pond. She carried her back to join Lunker for a feast of their favorite food.

Warren came to inform us that the ducks were doing just fine. "They've claimed this part of the grounds for their own because my ducks like it best closer to the house." He pointed to a pair of Peking ducks floating on the water beyond the footbridge. They were quite elegant, but neither of them had Lunker's alert curiosity. And neither of them had as perfect a topknot.

That visit made me feel much better about having left Lunker in the country. Finally I could wholeheartedly thank Pierre for finding them such a fabulous home.

Smiling, Pierre heaved a sigh and asked if we could get on with our lives. On the way home he announced that he had invited Margaret to tea.

When she arrived, before even thinking of sitting down, she toured the house and thoroughly inspected the garden, just in case I had hidden the ducks. Afterwards she stayed for the friendliest visit we had ever had from her and left for home satisfied.

The garden felt barren, as it might if all the trees had been cut down in one fell swoop.

During one of our trips to the country, Warren announced that Lunker was a female and apparently had mated with his Peking male. He figured all this out after discovering eggs in a nest on Lunker's territory.

I insisted that Lunker was definitely a male; therefore, the eggs must be Lunker's and Becky's.

"A Peking would never mate with an ordinary farm duck," Warren stated with authority, quickly adding that it didn't really matter anyway, because a creature had snuck in and stolen all the eggs. Stirring up some poison in a rusty pail, he strolled off to set it out for the thief. The knowledge that Lunker and Becky could mate successfully and lay a clutch of eggs pleased me.

I had several more good visits with the ducks, but in less than a month Becky behaved as though she didn't remember me. If I got close enough to pick her up, she would snuggle comfortably in my arms. But she usually preferred to remain at a distance; so Lunker received most of my attention. He loved it and never again made any moves to pinch me. The fact that both ducks were content in their new world alleviated my guilt for abandoning them.

Another a month had passed, I dreamed:

Lunker and I were in a lush green meadow filled with white daisies. Attempting to fly, Lunker wildly flapped his wings. Suddenly he managed to lift off and rise up about five feet in the air. As he flew away from me, I called out, "Lunker, oh Lunky love, Nancy loves you." He dipped one wing and awkwardly turned to fly straight into my arms.

Seeing Lunker airborne was a thrilling sight but even more exciting was to watch him fly towards me and to feel him land in my outstretched arms. His soft-feathered body pressed against me until he nestled inside my heart. Every cell in my body seemed to open to this sudden surge of love. It wasn't that I felt love for just Lunker, it was because of him that I opened up to a new dimension of love.

In the morning, the garden looked exceptionally beautiful. The rose bush was bursting with new buds. Whatever the dream meant, I felt elated until later that day when I found my only photograph of Lunker in the wastebasket. It had fallen off the wall beside my desk. I wondered if this meant Lunker was in trouble and needed my help.

CHAPTER 23

The Chicken Pen

As we approached Warren's place, the knot in my stomach grew bigger. I had no idea what I would find but feared it would be unpleasant. That's why I had persuaded Pierre to come with me.

After unlatching the gate and stepping inside, I quickly scanned the grounds and pond for Lunker.

He was nowhere in sight.

That wasn't unusual. What was strange however, was that after I sang our duet and called out for him a couple of times, he still didn't appear.

"Lunker, oh Lunky love..." I crooned in my most inviting voice while walking towards the shore of the pond where he especially liked to swim, but he never appeared.

It was Becky who darted out from behind a tree and frantically waddled up to me. In all the time she had been at Warren's she had never come to me on her own volition. She shook her head from side to side and made the weirdest sounds as she desperately tried to tell me something. Becky's distraught behavior supported my fear that Lunker was in trouble. With Lunker nowhere in sight, I wanted so badly to be able to understand Becky. The strange noises came from some dark chasm of despair. I recognized the source but couldn't decipher the message.

In the midst of my panic, I glanced up to see a scowling Warren march across the footpath towards us with his arms crossed tight against his chest.

"If you want to see your duck," he said nastily, "I've locked him up in the chicken pen."

Just to hear that Lunker was still alive filled me with relief.

"And if you don't want him harvested you'd better hurry up and find him a new home."

My impulse was to rush off to the chicken pen, but at the same time I feared doing anything that might make Warren angrier.

He ignored me while explaining to Pierre how Lunker had created havoc by going after his female Peking. And that wasn't the worst of it.

"Your damn duck" – now he was glaring at me – "He's taken to swimming across the pond whenever I'm in my garden. He sneaks up behind me to pinch my legs. He's downright vicious!"

"That's strange," I lied outright. "I can't imagine what's gotten into him." Before Pierre had a chance to say a word, I apologized to Warren, assured him that I would definitely find Lunker a new home and, without wasting another minute, ran off to the chicken pen to see how Lunker was faring.

Even though I imagined the worst, I still was not prepared for what I saw.

Locked up in a 5' x 5' grungy pen along with nine ill tempered, loudly clucking chickens, stood Lunker all covered with mud. While I watched, several of the chickens plucked Lunker's gorgeous tail feathers and dropped them in the mud where more of his feathers were scattered.

When he saw me, Lunker strutted over to the chicken wire with his head held high; his aristocratic nature managed somehow to shine through the mud. He looked at me as if to ask what had taken me so long to get there. The reason for his confinement totally bewildered him. He flashed me an angry look as though it was my fault that he was locked up with such mean, filthy creatures.

While I tried to figure out how to get past the pecking chickens in order to free Lunker, Pierre appeared and handed me an open can of sardines. But each time I tried to slip some through the wire to Lunker, a chicken would lunge and snatch it while another chicken attacked Lunker from behind.

Pierre figured out that if he gave a good portion of the sardines directly to the chickens I could slip a generous helping to Lunker. It worked. But when I asked him how I could get Lunker out of the pen without being attacked, he reminded me that we had just settled things with our landlady.

"Margaret will kick us out if you bring Lunker back to the house. Don't even entertain the idea. I'm not about to lose my home because of a duck. Besides," Pierre added a bit more gently, "Have you forgotten that we're leaving soon on our trip to Wisconsin?"

I was stunned. "Surely you don't expect me to leave him here to be slaughtered."

His assurance that Lunker had lived a good life didn't appease me. "Better than any duck I've ever known," he persisted. "Warren won't kill him right off, he'll wait a bit to see if you find a place for him."

Even though I couldn't fathom Lunker spending yet another night in the chicken pen, I knew Pierre was right. I couldn't bring Lunker back home.

We had been planning our return to Pierre's family farm for more than a year. Many of the farms in the Midwest were in serious trouble, and it was quite possible that Pierre's brother might soon have to sell. It wouldn't have been fair to Pierre to suddenly change my mind.

Because I didn't think I could ever find him another paradise I bawled Lunker out. He listened. Through his mud-caked face his eyes seemed to shine more lustrously than ever.

For Lunker, who took such pride in his pristine appearance, it was torturous to have to stand around in the chicken's filth while covered with mud himself.

I told him to hang in there, I'd be back first thing in the morning. The look he gave me as I turned to walk away was heart wrenching.

By the time we passed Becky on our way to the gate, she had calmed down. Apparently she felt much better now that I was aware of Lunker's plight.

I plotted his rescue during the drive home. No matter what Pierre thought, I knew that there was really very little time. Warren had made it perfectly clear that he would take great pleasure in harvesting my duck.

I spent the entire afternoon phoning everyone I could think of just in case they might know of a place for the ducks. Not one person could help me out.

As I collapsed beside the phone with my head in my hands trying to figure out what to do next, Carla arrived, filling the room with her teenage exuberance.

"How soon do you have to find them a new place?" she asked after I explained my dilemma.

"By morning," I told her.

"Oh that is a bit quick," she laughed and told me to stop worrying. She promised to find the ducks a new home and raced out the door.

That night Pierre went to bed early. I paced the bedroom in the dark. The moment I heard the front door open, I ran down the stairs. Carla flung her arms around my neck as soon as I reached the landing.

"Well, I did it," she beamed. Her new boyfriend's uncle had a farm about five miles beyond Warren's on the other side of the highway.

"He said he wouldn't mind having two more ducks. He has eleven already. Though let me warn you, Mom, this place is nothing like what they've been used to. I mean its kind of funky. But there's a pond."

I was greatly relieved. No matter what it was like it would save Lunker from being slaughtered. I thanked Carla profusely for agreeing to get up early and drive out with me to rescue the ducks.

The night seemed endless. I kept waking up, imagining Lunker surrounded by those chickens, his eyes shining through the darkness.

CHAPTER 24

Rescuing Lunker

When morning finally came, Carla and I skipped breakfast, tossed a big cardboard box in the car, and left much earlier than planned. I couldn't wait to free Lunker. We sailed down the highway with our hair blowing in the wind.

Becky was standing under a tree, as distraught as ever, but no longer making those strange frantic sounds. Instead she silently dipped her head from side to side stopping only long enough to walk around in circles.

We ran straight to the chicken pen. It was a relief to find Lunker alive. He was a bit muddier and missing a few more tail feathers, but my promise that I would rescue him must have kept his spirits up. He was standing beside the fence in the same spot where I had left him.

Carla found a big stick on the ground, unlatched the hook on the door to the pen, and stormed in swinging the stick. While she crowded the chickens to the rear corner, distracting them, I rushed in behind her and snatched up Lunker. Holding him at arm's length, I slid through the mud as I scrambled out of the pen.

While I carried him to the pond, Lunker began singing happily. Holding him by the neck, I dipped him into the water and swished him around. When I pulled him out, he was wet and white. He loved it. He flashed me an adoring glance. He would have let me swing him around by one leg, flip him upside down, or push his head under water. He didn't care. He had escaped the chicken pen. Once the mud was off his feathers, he became the handsome Lunker again, the aristocratic duck, in spite of his missing tail feathers.

With bewildered fascination Becky stood under a tree out of reach watching me bathe Lunker. Every time Carla got close, Becky would run off. She was afraid of being caught. She trusted no one. But once we circled her, and Carla managed to grab her, Becky snuggled up in her arms, while Lunker sat in the box in the middle of the front seat right beside me and with great pleasure watched the trees zip past the car window.

I never did see Warren that morning, but it was just as well. What could I have said? I didn't feel like thanking him.
As we traveled down the road, I sang, "Oh, we saved you from the chicken pen!" Lunker, all white and clean and oh so pleased to be sitting beside me, answered with more gusto than ever before, "Babop, babop, babop." He gazed at me with pure devotion.

That was before he realized that we weren't taking him back to the garden where he had reigned as king. When I asked Carla if her boyfriend's uncle knew that Lunker and Becky were male and female, she said she hadn't mentioned it and that he had never asked. She told me that he might be assuming they were both females. That was his preference since he had nine males already.

I didn't even want to think about it.

Lunker kept singing. In his mind, he was going home!

CHAPTER 25

Five Hefty Farm Ducks

As we drove up the driveway to the farm, I instantly understood what Carla had meant when she referred to it as “funky." It was cluttered with junk, old rusty equipment, and piles of used tires.

We walked around, looking things over while waiting for the owner to appear. The ducks followed our every step. When Carla pointed out the pond, which was nice and big but had very steep embankments, Lunker headed straight for the water. It had been quite some time since he'd had a chance to swim.

Before he was even halfway down the embankment, five hefty farm ducks swam across the pond and charged after him. Lunker could hardly scramble up fast enough to escape. Becky watched all of this from the rim along with Carla and me. That one incident quickly informed all four of us whose territory this was.

The owner, a weathered old man, soon approached and assured me that the ducks would be fed and given lots of affection. Something about the tone of his voice made me doubt this. He never asked if the ducks were male or female, and we didn't offer the information.

When a light rain began to fall, we decided it was a good time to leave and let the ducks explore their new home on their own, to settle in as best they could.

"Don't worry, Mom," Carla said trying to reassure me that the other ducks would accept Lunker once they got used to him. But we both knew he might have to win a few fights first. Good as Lunker was at charging and pinching, I wondered about his ability to battle it out with another duck, let alone nine of them. Yet, I felt I had no choice but to leave him there. I tried to convince myself that this farm was a better place for him and Becky to live than in town in my little garden. Our bathtub couldn't compare to a pond.

I consoled myself with the fact that Lunker had Becky. Carla slid her arm through mine and told me that the quicker we left, the easier it would be. As we walked toward the car, Lunker stood in the driveway watching us go in utter disbelief. In his mind the farm had just been a brief stop. We couldn't possibly be leaving him behind.

He watched us get into the car. I turned my face away. When I finally glanced into the rearview mirror, I saw that he hadn't moved. His eye was still on me.

* * *

During the following week, because there was no phone call from the farm informing us of any trouble, I assumed that Becky and Lunker were all right. I purposely waited a while before returning to visit, in order to give the ducks a chance to adapt to their new surroundings without interference from me.

When Jennifer and I arrived at the farm, Lunker was sitting in the same spot I had left him in. He turned his head away when he saw me. He did the same when I offered him sardines. It didn't occur to either of us to sing.

Becky waddled around nearby keeping an eye on us but stayed a safe distance away. Jennifer tried to catch her with no luck at all, so she went off to find the owner. In a few minutes she returned with a full report.

He had said that Lunker and Becky would be allowed to swim in the pond only when Lunker was willing to fight the head honcho and his cohorts. But so far Lunker hadn't shown any interest in battling it out.

Jenny also mentioned that apparently Lunker spent a lot of time sitting in the driveway listening and waiting for my car. That explained why he looked so dusty and despondent. When I tried to talk to him, he behaved indifferently towards me. I knew it was pretense. He was terribly hurt, incredibly angry.

It was easy to understand how the other male ducks would be jealous of handsome Lunker. Because he could look like an aristocrat even when dirty, he made the other ducks feel ordinary. Obviously they were guarding their territory and keeping any potential competition away from their females. I wondered what would happen if one of the males took an interest in Becky.

I picked Lunker up and held him in my arms. He hung his head over my shoulder and whimpered as he had while grieving the death of Little Guy.

My knees began to tremble. I set him down and turned to walk away. When we drove off, I knew I wouldn't be seeing Lunker for more than a month. I had to remind myself that it was he who had blown it at Warren's. During the time I spent preparing for our forthcoming trip to Wisconsin, I kept hoping that Lunker would gradually learn to like his new home.

I had expended so much emotion over Lunker that I finally reached a dry spell. I often thought about him, but I could no longer bear to suffer because of him. I wanted to be in good spirits when Pierre and I journeyed back to the place where we had spent our first glorious summer together.

As Pierre packed the last of our things into the trunk of the car, I asked Jennifer and Carla to visit the ducks while we were gone. Lunker and Becky needed to know that they hadn't been forgotten. I told the girls that I would phone periodically to find out how they were faring and to get a report on the ducks.

"When you visit Lunker, please stroke his neck and say in a sweet voice, "Oh Lunker, oh Lunky love, Nancy loves you." Please do it, no matter how silly you feel. He needs to know that I care about him even when I'm not coming to see him. Will you do that for me?"

Carla and Jennifer both nodded gravely.

CHAPTER 26

We Visit Wisconsin

In Wisconsin, on the land where Pierre had spent his childhood, the sumac had already turned a brilliant red. We couldn't have chosen a better time to be there. The days were sunny and the evenings balmy. We awoke every morning to race down the grassy hill and dive into the cold, clear lake. I couldn't help thinking what a perfect place it would be for Lunker and Becky if someone was there all the time to look after them.

Pierre and I went raspberry picking, hiked through the wildflowers in the meadows, and lay down every now and then in a deer bed to rest. We laughed a lot like young lovers. We chopped wood, dug potatoes and every three days, we took sauna.

The bank had come through and re-mortgaged the farm so it was out of danger, at least for the time being. For an entire week nothing troubled us. No one phoned. We didn't once turn on the radio, and there wasn't any television. Pierre and I never even felt the urge to drive into town to buy a newspaper.

When I phoned to check on the girls, I learned that all was well, and heard the good news that the ducks had built a nest behind the barn where Becky laid another clutch of eggs. They also told me that whenever the other ducks left the pond to go eat, Lunker and Becky would sneak down to the water for a quick swim. Such good news abated my fear that Lunker was miserable.

A few more days passed. After taking sauna we walked in the moonlight down the path to Pierre's grandfather's cottage. Fireflies danced all around us. Almost as soon as we climbed into the big maple bed, I fell into a luscious deep sleep. Around midnight I had a terrible dream:

> *I was being hunted in the woods by a group of men with guns. When they surrounded me and pointed their weapons at my heart, I felt like a helpless deer with no escape. I experienced the terror that every hunted animal and every creature facing slaughter feels.*

I awoke in a cold sweat. Pierre heard my fearful cry. He held me and stroked my hair. The full moon shone in the window and lit the room. I felt overwhelmed by a fear that Lunker had been "harvested." Pierre tried to tell me it was just a nightmare. But the dream and Lunker's death were connected. I knew it. I could feel it in my bones.

Early the next morning, I phoned the girls and asked as casually as I could whether they had been to visit Lunker recently. To my surprise they assured me all was well. Becky's eggs had hatched and she was now swimming in the pond with little Lunkers close behind.

While we lay on the dock to sun ourselves and watch the light dance on the lake, a mother duck and her four chicks glided out from the tall reeds a few feet away to swim towards us. For an instant, I no longer saw the mottled grey-brown fuzzy chicks I had been watching; instead, I saw them as yellow, each with a little cotton ball puff perched on top of its head.

* * *

Pierre and I spent our last day at the cottage dragging down the fallen maple trees from the hillside forest and chopping them up to replenish the wood supply for the sauna. At the end of the day, we fell into the featherbed more than pleased with our vacation. The same night I had the following dream:

> *I was standing by the lakeshore in front of the cottage with the yellow leaves from the poplar fluttering down on me. As I looked up at the tree, I saw a golden bird perched on a branch but he quickly flew away. A few minutes later, when I glanced back up into the poplar, I noticed that the bird had returned. This time he flew towards me, but just before reaching me, veered away and flew back to the tree. He did this several times until finally he snuggled inside my blouse and pressed his soft feathers against my bare skin right at my heart. At first I worried that the bird might crush himself or hurt his wings but he snuggled even closer and made himself quite comfortable. At that point it felt right for the golden bird to be there. In a flash, he had entered the*

very core of my being. I knew somehow that my soul had flown home.

All the next day I felt strong, at peace, whole. Yet I knew that this dream experience couldn't have happened if I hadn't known and loved Lunker. It was very much like the dream of Lunker opening my heart.

As we traveled home, I grew more and more excited over the approaching reunion with my daughters and with Lunker. After such a rejuvenating trip with Pierre, I felt blessed to have two daughters and a duck awaiting my return.

Upon our arrival, Jennifer and Carla rushed out to greet us. I plopped down on the couch to catch my breath. Within seconds, I sensed that something was drastically wrong. Even though they both tried to hide it, disaster was written all over their faces.

CHAPTER 27

The News

"Okay, what happened? What are you hiding? Come on, tell me. Get it over with."

The way Pierre shrugged and said, "I'm sure it will keep until morning," I knew he also suspected the worst.

Their silence had already said it.

With forced cheerfulness Carla began to tell me how cute Becky's four little ducklings were with topknots just like Lunker's. Jennifer nodded frantically.

I said, "He's dead isn't he? Lunker's dead."

Jennifer began to cry. She said they didn't know what exactly had happened.

"He died sitting in the driveway," Carla said bleakly.

"He just got sick and died, I guess."

"Maybe his life span was over," Pierre suggested. "Ducks don't live forever, you know."

Carla and Jennifer both confessed that they had lied to me on the phone, because they didn't want to spoil our vacation. "There wasn't anything you could do about it anyway," Carla said.

* * *

The loss of Lunker left me numb at first, then it began to hurt. I realized that I didn't know the first thing about dealing with grief. I couldn't bear to be out in the garden, everything reminded me of him. I vowed never to play my flute again. The same question kept torturing me. How could I have abandoned him after so much love had passed between us?

Pierre was annoyed with what he called my "over-reacting," but he tried to console me all the same by assuring me the pain would lessen with time.

I couldn't believe it. Not to be able to sit beside him, never to sing with him again, never to run my fingers down his back, feeling the velvety touch of his soft white feathers.

CHAPTER 28

Back in the Garden

Periodically, Jennifer went to check on Becky and her brood, who were thriving, but I never returned. I didn't want to be anywhere near the place where Lunker died, nor did I feel a need to know the details of his death. I struggled not to suspect the worst. At the same time, I feared that he had caused some sort of trouble, and he had ended up as someone's supper.

I knew that if I saw Lunker's ducklings I would climb down the embankment myself, capture every one of them, and Becky too, and bring them home to my garden, where I would make a pond and feed them sardines every night.

Imagine. Little Lunkers.

* * *

Several weeks passed before I could force myself to go out and actually sit in the garden. I placed the lawn chair in the very spot where I had consoled Lunker after Little Guy's death. As I stared at the neglected rose bush, I remembered Lunker's mourning sounds and could almost feel his beak nestled in the hair at the nape of my neck. This helped release my tears. It felt good to give in to my sorrow.

As the tears subsided, I glanced over at the spot under the poplar seedling where Lunker liked to sit. For a moment, I thought I saw a gorgeous white feather lying there. It couldn't possibly be his. Surely, I would have noticed it long before. I jumped up and ran over to discover that it was indeed one of Lunker's feathers.

That night, after climbing into bed, I slipped the feather under my pillow. While I slept, Lunker paid me a visit:

He was a bit older and somewhat scragglier. He sat down beside me. I stroked his back and ruffled his neck feathers, while we sang our duet.

In the morning, Hummer was flitting from flower to flower up and down the flame vine outside my window. As I watched this tiny creature with fascination, I knew that my relationship to Lunker had bonded my soul to birds. What I didn't know at the time was that another bird would soon be flying into my life.

CHAPTER 29

A Whole Chorus of Birds...

The entire time that Lunker was in my life, I had continued working on the novel with a sense that our relationship would bring forth the kind of insight I needed to complete my book. But it was too early to assimilate what I was experiencing.

Because the novel was also my M.F.A. thesis, the pressure of knowing my writing was going to be judged often left me frozen until the last few weeks when I absolutely had to make progress; after which I wrote twelve hours a day. Long before the book was due, I felt as if all creativity had been drained out of me.

At 5:00 a.m. on the morning of the deadline, after I had slept only four hours, a chorus of birds awakened me. It was well before dawn and never before at that hour had I heard birds singing. Their loud songs wouldn't allow me to fall back asleep. I remember thinking to myself, ‘Well, if the birds are here to get me up, they must want this book to be finished.’

Once again, I sat myself in front of the typewriter and saw my way through terror and a blinding migraine that began flashing around noon. I kept on writing until I took a break for a bath that prepared me for the final push. Even though Gloria succeeded in confronting the "turkey man” at an Indian ritual she had been invited to, I knew that there was some old terror of mine that I hadn't yet released.

I made my thesis deadline. But the birds that had come to wake me up that morning had joined a chorus of other messenger birds appearing in my life. Would they lead to the discovery of deeper missing truths?

CHAPTER 30
Sadat

At the same time that I began to write about Lunker's death, a bird struck our window with such force it sounded like a sonic boom. Only his feathers prevented the glass from shattering

I raced out the bedroom door and down the stairs dreading the probability that I would find a dead or injured bird.

On an impulse, I rushed across the patio to look into the fountain. There I found a little mourning dove frantically flapping his wings in a desperate attempt to stay afloat.

I lifted him out of the water and held him in my hand. The only touches of color on this bird were a few dusty-rose wing feathers and his tiny piercing red eyes. While perched on my finger, he made no attempt to fly off. His mottled grey feathers began to dry and fluff up. That is when I noticed how one of his wings hung lower than the other. I couldn't be sure however, whether it was broken or whether he couldn't fly because he was still a fledgling. I had recently read an article that said never put a wing in a sling because there is a good chance that it will heal by itself in nine days.

Nine days, I kept thinking. Would I be able to keep this bird alive for nine days?

I called to Jennifer to come hold the dove while I cooked an egg and mushed it together with oatmeal and water; then she dashed off to buy an eyedropper at the drugstore.

After we fed him, I dunked his beak into a shot glass full of water to see if he would drink by himself. A drop of blood slid out into the glass. I wondered if he had suffered a concussion. Jennifer and I both feared the dove wouldn't make it through the night, but neither of us admitted our doubts.

She found a shoebox and padded it with a piece of flannel before we set the bird inside. We draped the scarf that had been used on Becky's box over the shoebox which we put in a dark corner of the bedroom where it would be safe for the dove to sleep.

I checked in on him an hour later. He was sitting perfectly still with his eyes closed. I touched him with my hand to make sure his body was warm. I kept thinking, *nine days*.

That night when Pierre came home, I told him how amazed I had been by the mysterious impulse that had led me to the dove. Without even thinking, I had run across the patio straight to the fountain. This reminded Pierre of an experience his grandmother had in France when he was a boy.

One day while scrubbing floors, she suddenly leapt to her feet, ran down the stairs, out the front door and across the street to an empty lot. In an open cistern she saw a little girl dangling from the edge, hanging on by her fingertips. The drop into the deep water was more than twenty feet. Pierre's grandmother didn't understand what had prompted her to run to the cistern. She hadn't heard anyone scream or shout. She concluded that she must have been sent to pull the girl out.

Early the next morning as soon as I awoke, I rushed over to the shoebox to lift the scarf. What a joy it was to see the bird's eyes blink open. The sad intensity in his crimson-colored eyes reminded me of the Egyptian President Anwar Sadat, who had devoted his brilliance to world peace and had been assassinated. In his honor, I named the mourning dove, Sadat.

After feeding him mush and water with the eyedropper, I set Sadat on the patio beneath the fountain next to a potted rose bush so he wouldn't feel totally exposed. Then I sprinkled a handful of sesame seeds beside him.

I tried to touch him as little as possible hoping the other mourning doves would accept him back if he managed to fly off. I soon discovered that having a small wounded bird in my garden was quite a different experience from having an assertive duck who could easily protect himself. I knew that if I wanted Sadat to be free out in nature I would have to watch over him constantly.

I hadn't spent any time in the garden since Lunker died, nor had I played my flute, because I couldn't bear to be reminded of him. Whenever I thought of Lunker, I felt overwhelmed by grief. Who could I expect to understand or share it, when even I thought it ridiculous to be flooded by such intense emotion over the death of a duck? It seemed strange that Sadat would arrive in my life just when I tried for the first time to write about Lunker. I began to think that if I couldn't let go of a duck, how would I ever be able to say goodbye to Carla who would soon be leaving home to go to school in California. I felt grateful for this bird who needed my total attention.

The entire day, I sat in the lawn chair watching over Sadat. For hours at a time he just soaked up the sun without moving. At first I felt restless and impatient, but after a while I began to ease into reverie. Maybe the dove had come to show me that one must rest calmly in order to heal. The garden soon became a comfort to both of us.

Sadat liked to watch Ralph, an emerald-green lizard who slithered up and down the wall working his way closer to the dove; but mostly Sadat just sat quietly with his eyes shut. Ralph, who had lost his tail while escaping the claws of a cat, seemed intrigued with this gentle presence in the garden.

As the sun set, I fed Sadat with the eyedropper and put him in the box for the night. While Pierre and I were at the movies, I kept telling myself that Sadat could die at any time. When we returned home, I went instantly to the bedroom to lift the scarf. In the dark, I touched him. My fear dissolved when I felt Sadat was warm and breathing.

By the next morning Sadat refused to eat from the eyedropper. I put the mush on the tip of my tongue; he took it from between my lips with his beak. I don't know if I read somewhere how to do that or if I had instinctively become his mother. When his little beak pushed in and out of my lips, it tickled.

After I set him on the patio, Sadat scurried over to his sacred spot next to the potted rose bush. I put wheat berries in a jar lid and tossed seeds beside him thinking maybe his relatives would fly down to eat. I hoped that when they discovered him they would keep him company until he was able to go off with them.

Sadat seemed happy to be alive there in the garden. After my experience with Gilguerro, it amazed me that Sadat remained so calm. I told myself that if it was true that it takes nine days for a wing to mend, Sadat had only seven more days to wait.

While watching over him, I learned how to sit still and listen. Sometimes the sounds of San Miguel would flow right through me, the chink, chink, chink of a hammer against stone, a truck grinding up the cobblestone hill, a dog barking in the distance, laughter from two women across the street, and church bells very far away. I knew the only reason I heard these sounds was because I had been listening.

Memories of my seventeen years with Carla flashed vividly through my mind. I saw her, at two years old, riding down the grassy hill on the back of the Norwegian Elkhound.

She clutched his fur, squealing with delight, until she fell off and rolled down the hill laughing.

I saw us alone in the car in the middle of a freezing Minnesota night. I was terrified but trying to calm her while I drove as fast as I dared to the emergency room. Seven-year-old Carla was wrapped in a blanket beside me, gasping for breath in the midst of an asthma attack.

"Are you warm enough?" she asked as she covered my legs with part of her blanket.

She was performing in the grade school talent show wearing the huge paper maché chicken head we had made. In the midst of her hilarious act, she stepped right off the front of the stage. I leapt out of my chair and raced up to see if she was injured. She was all right but terribly embarrassed.

"We put the eyeholes in the wrong place," she explained.

On her twelfth birthday, she was performing once again. No longer the clumsy nine-year-old, she was a lithe and graceful ballerina. With glowing pride, I watched her glide through the air leaping and spinning.

It has been said that when you die your past reels before you like a filmstrip. Maybe because our relationship as we had always known it was ending, memories of our life together were reeling off in my head.

Hummer appeared; flitted nearby, showing off. He knew he was the only bird who could hover in mid-air and fly backwards.

Sadat ignored him and continued to eat his seeds. For the first time since he had been in my garden, Sadat began preening. He fanned out his wings as if to display his dusty-rose feathers. At first I thought he was listening to the Gregorian chants on the tape deck while catching flies but soon realized he was probably concentrating on their buzz.

When Margaret's yellow angora cat crept across the roof tiles in hopes of having *bird* for supper, I chased her away with the broom. Afterwards I worried that maybe I had frightened Sadat by such aggression. He always perked up when he heard the seven mourning doves cooing from the nearby peppercorn tree while they tenderly preened one another.

On Sadat's third day, the miracle I had hoped for happened, but not in the way I had wanted it to. A mourning dove flew down to eat the seed. When he got close enough to Sadat, he viciously pecked at him until I rushed over to chase him away.

Sadat stood with his beak parted, gasping all afternoon. I wondered if he would live through the day. It was a matter of spirit. How strange to think that the sound of wings had become a threat to Sadat.

On the fourth morning, Sadat was not only alive, but feisty! As I carried him downstairs to the garden, he pecked at my hand. When I set him in Lunker's grass patch, he went right for the poplar seedling and stood beside the base of the trunk. His feathers were the exact same grey as the bark. This new territory frightened him.

I gave him a few drops of water from the eyedropper, though he seemed to think it ridiculous that I still treated him like such a baby. After I set him back down, he scooted along the grass to stand beside the tall green stem of the white iris.

Carla came out into the garden and looked wistfully at this bird I was nurturing. I gave Carla the purple satin shoes and fancy glittery socks I had been saving for when she left for college.

"We grew up together. That's what makes it so hard to leave," she said as we hugged each other.

The next morning Sadat was eager to get outside. He still couldn't fly but was so chipper and happy. I painted the windowpanes, trying to accomplish something in the house while at the same time keeping a constant eye on him. Several times I had to race out to the garden to scare away a cat or one of the pecking mourning doves.

That night I put the shoebox in Jenny's room so Sadat could sleep without breathing any paint fumes.

On the sixth day, Sadat looked terribly thin. But I knew that he had been eating because there were several droppings in the shoebox. I had to go to town for a while, so I tried to put Sadat back into the box. He ran away from me to hide in the woodpile where I couldn't get at him. The entire time away, I was frantic with worry that a cat would get him. When I arrived home, Sadat was standing in the center of the patio waiting for me. As soon as he saw me, he ran off to the potting corner where he knew I could catch him.

Late that afternoon, I raced out to chase an attacking bird and discovered that Sadat was nowhere in sight. I looked all over to see if he was lying somewhere pecked to death. Finally, I found him hiding beside the tree. He wouldn't scoot over to the food dish to eat his fill until I was right there to protect him.

Sadat jumped out of my hands when he thought I was going to put him in the shoebox. He still couldn't fly, but he managed to spread his wings and glide six inches off the ground until he reached the grass patch where he landed. He ran so fast to the woodpile, I couldn't catch him. In an hour, he came out, squeaking loud enough to let me know he was ready to be caught and taken in for the night.

On the seventh day, I began to wonder if Sadat would ever be able to fly. He had figured out by now that if he stayed hidden among the irises and daisies, I wouldn't bother him, and the mourning doves who flew down to eat his food wouldn't attack him.

When we reached the garden that morning, he sprang out of my hands again. Spreading his wings, he glided to the ground. I knew he didn't like spending his nights in the shoebox any more, but I couldn't let him go free until he was able to fly and protect himself.

It was wonderful to have another feathered friend in my garden. I felt grateful that he diverted my attention from the pain of Lunker's death and Carla's forthcoming departure. I, of course, was becoming very attached to Sadat, but I didn't want to become possessive this time. I would guard over him until he healed, then help him fly away safely. I didn't want to domesticate him or have him become reliant on me. Yet, after seven days, I had begun to count on his presence.

I considered banding his leg so that when he did leave I could look into the tree and positively identify him.

Since Sadat's arrival, this was the first day I felt free to write. He was sunning and able to scoot over to the woodpile to hide if he needed to. That day Pierre said, "I'm afraid to tell you this, but it's very possible that Sadat will never fly again."

I held Sadat on my finger. He cocked his head to look at me. He seemed to sniff the air but didn't attempt to fly. I began to think that maybe he didn't know how. Maybe Sadat never had broken his wing. Late that afternoon, as I stood on the upstairs balcony, I saw another cat sneaking across the roof with his eye on Sadat. Without thinking, I picked up a huge rock and threw it at the cat. It missed but smashed a skylight in Margaret's storage cottage. I felt like a delinquent adolescent, but at the same time something besides the glass broke.

My anger towards Margaret for demanding I find Lunker a new home was suddenly released. It felt good to hurl that rock, and even better when the window shattered.

***

On the morning of the ninth day, I held Sadat on my finger while I stood on the stairs trying to coax him to fly. He trembled at the prospect of leaping off my finger into the air. I moved my face closer and closer towards him threatening to kiss his feathers if he didn't fly. He waited until just before my lips touched him before he sprang off and at the same time fanned out his wings. Gracefully, he glided down to the grass patch.

I went into the house to make a pot of tea, and when I came back outside, Sadat was gone. I could only hope he was hiding in the woodpile.

The longer he stayed away, the more I worried that a cat might have caught him. Four hours later he reappeared on the patio, much to my relief.

When it began to grow dark and time for him to sleep, he hid in the woodpile and made it impossible for me to bring him inside for the night. I slept fitfully, roused by every strange sound.

Morning finally came, and I rushed outside to see if he was all right. I peered into the woodpile and heard a flapping of wings. Sadat flew off to the potting corner where I caught him and held him on my finger. What a joy. He was really on his own.

Later that same day, Carla and I watched from the window as Sadat made friends with a mourning dove who came to eat from his dish.

Margaret's cat stood beside the water dish smelling bird, but Sadat hid between the iris and the wall. Ralph watched. Hummer also. Sadat behaved like a full-grown bird that day in his actions and in the way he carried himself.

He flew from my finger while I stood on the upstairs balcony, but he landed in the fountain again. I rushed down and pulled him out of the water. He looked so bewildered with his little red eyes blinking. Later, coaxed by my threat to kiss him, he showed Carla how he could fly.

Sadat spent the night once again in the woodpile. Just before I turned off the patio light to go to bed, I saw both of Margaret's cats stalking around.

In the morning, two doves were sitting under the pomegranate tree. Was one of them Sadat?

As I came within two feet of the birds, they both flew off. When I crouched down and saw Sadat on the woodpile, he managed to lift off but couldn't quite make it into the air as high as the roof. Instead he landed on the wall that enclosed the garden. It was the very first time I saw him take off from the ground and fly on his own. Sadat sat on the ledge for a good long while looking at me. Then he flew back down to the grass patch.

Later that same afternoon, Sadat flew off again and landed successfully in the peppercorn tree beyond the garden. I began crying for the loss of him, for the loss of Lunker, and for the forthcoming loss of Carla from my life. When the tears subsided, I felt released.

Several days later I watched Sadat join a dove couple as they preened on the roof. I discovered then that there was no need to band him; I could easily distinguish which mourning dove was Sadat.

Every once in a while the couple would include him in their preening. Gracefully, Sadat fanned out his wing, displaying his rosy feathers.

Every morning I put seed out on a ledge on the upstairs balcony, and Sadat flew in with a few other doves to eat. One day as I watched him, I heard a distant rooster crow; the red house finch singing his heart out; Hummer was there also, sucking nectar out of the flaming vine flowers. Everything felt glorious in the garden that morning. Even the crimson roses were in full bloom.

CHAPTER 31

Hummer in the Yucatan

Just before Carla was to leave for the states, Pierre and I decided to take a trip to the Yucatan to gather material for a film script we were collaborating on. It was an exciting and successful journey. After working diligently for several days, we rewarded ourselves with a visit to *Isla de Mujeres*, Island of Women. It was there that Hummer appeared in my dream:

> *While I was on the telephone unable to decipher an urgent message, I noticed Hummer's head lying beside me on the floor. For some reason I picked it up, put it in my mouth, and immediately became hysterical. My sister said, 'Don't carry on like that, it doesn't help.' I took Hummer's head out of my mouth, held it in my hand and watched as he gradually became whole again. I knew he was trying desperately to warn me about something.*

While we were on the island, we spent some time in the crumbling stone temple, which had been an ancient menstrual hut. There we chanted and said prayers to the Great Goddess. I asked for the power to let my children go and the courage to trust my own voice.

With waves crashing against the rocks below the cliff which the hut was perched on, with the full moon high in the sky, with my blood flowing, as I sat in this ancient Woman space, I felt a power rushing through me that I had never before experienced. For the first time I felt totally in tune with the elements. We chanted for a long while. At one point I could hear a bell-like tone escaping from deep inside my throat.

We returned to San Miguel to learn that Margaret had sold the house. Within the next three days, Carla left home and the Mexican banks confiscated most of our money with their drastic devaluation.

I wasn't at all prepared for what I would feel that day. I held Carla in my arms, and kissed her goodbye. My heart was tearing. If Lunker had not come into my life so that I would experience the first shock of loss; if Sadat hadn't come to show me that I could care for something, and that even though I let it fly free it would return to my garden, I might not have believed that Carla would return after her journey out into the world.

Because I was so emotionally involved with Carla's departure, it took a while to realize that when we left the house I would also be leaving Sadat and Hummer behind. The thought of a life without them was more painful than letting go of the house I had loved more than any other.

CHAPTER 32

Sadat, again...

A couple of days before we actually moved out, I was exhausted from packing. Because I slept so late, Sadat's breakfast seed didn't get put on the patio ledge at the usual time. While I was sitting on the stool in the bathroom half asleep, I heard the whirrrrrr of wings and looked up to see that Sadat had flown through the open door into the bathroom with several doves behind him. I counted seventeen of them. When the other birds saw me, they looked a bit freaked, as if they were wondering why Sadat would lead them so close to a human.

Because the upstairs bathroom looked out upon the tops of flowering trees, we often left the door open. It was especially lovely to soak in a hot bath while gazing out at the potted plants on the patio, and beyond, past the trees to a vast and almost always sunny sky.

Sadat flew in, gave me a good long look, dropped to the floor and proceeded to scoot under the bathroom sink where I kept his seed up above in a drawer. Some of the seed had fallen through a crack onto the floor. The other doves followed him staying as far away from me as possible while they ate all the seeds they could find. I sat very still watching their bobbing heads.

CHAPTER 33

Paloma

We moved to the house that Lorena and Carl had lived in before they left for the States, taking Far Out with them. I couldn’t bear the dust that constantly made my eyes itch. I felt a tremendous sadness I couldn't shake and never did find a space to write in. I spent a lot of time weeding the garden, all the while hoping that somehow Hummer and Sadat might find me, but it never happened.

Just when I began to accept the fact that birds had left my life forever, Pierre discovered a bedraggled mourning dove hiding behind a potted plant. The dove had managed to stay alive in spite of the numerous cats constantly prowling around. He couldn't fly and didn't take an interest in preening himself or even in eating. I knew right away that Paloma didn't have the same will to live as Sadat. Or maybe she was lacking Sadat's wisdom.

Someone once told me that there is a tribe in South America where women put eggs between their breasts because it is the perfect temperature for hatching. This gave me the idea to make a little pouch out of a scarf, where Paloma could spend a lot of time sleeping next to my breast. It seemed to be the only place where she felt comfortable.

Within a few days she died. While digging the hole in the ground, I felt as if my ability to save birds had vanished. A couple of neighbor children watched me bury Paloma and were soon bringing dead animals over to put in the ground next to her. One child even brought a cat that had been rotting in the alley. Another brought a baby duckling that had recently died.

Before long, I had created another burial ground.

CHAPTER 34

From Here to There

One afternoon, as we were running errands in preparation to leave San Miguel, we were detained outside of town by a funeral procession. All the women were weeping and even the men were crying, which is quite unusual in Mexico. It is not that they don't grieve, but death is very much a part of life to them. They don't hide it or refer to it with euphemisms. Instead, every year they celebrate the Day of the Dead by taking flowers and food to the cemetery where they party all night long with the spirits of their departed relatives and friends.

As the procession passed us, we saw the reason for their extreme sadness. In the open casket lay a young woman, and in her arms, a newborn child.

When you see a corpse before your very eyes, you feel small for bewailing the mere pain of separation you have been experiencing. Yet you also know that your loss carries with it an intimation of the final ultimate death. That is why it hurts the way it does. It connects you with death in its totality.

Death becomes the myth you are living.

This vision of the dead mother and child put my sadness and loss into perspective and made me feel fortunate that Carla was out in the world alive and well and that I still had three more years with Jennifer.

Shortly before returning to Minnesota, I had a vivid dream that was also a very physical experience:

I was stepping from one world into another. There were two spheres suspended in the sky, and as my forward foot left the one sphere, I slipped into nowhere, a place without space and time. I had definitely left the old life but hadn't yet entered the new.

I thought about this dream, and worried that it might be predicting a possible plane crash. I feared its purpose was to prepare me for leaving life while caught between two worlds. After this fear subsided, I began to wonder if the feeling I had in the dream is how we feel when we die.

This thought left me with a new perspective on death. Maybe it could be as easy as stepping from here to there.

My experience of moving from one country to another was accurately depicted in that dream, maybe because the Latin-American culture is so different from ours

When I am in Mexico, I can't quite visualize Minnesota. It becomes as hazy as the past. Even snow becomes an abstraction. While trying to recall the scent of Minnesota pines and the wet fertile earth in the spring, I could only smell the scent of night-blooming jasmine.

Once back in Minnesota, the years spent in Mexico seemed as remote as if they had happened in someone else's life, or at least in an old incarnation. My eyes couldn't see past the steel-grey winter sky to conjure up the rosy glow at dusk that exudes from the rocks and walls in San Miguel.

CHAPTER 35

The Great Blue Heron

It was wonderful coming home to Minnesota. We found a great house on Lake Carnelian about seven miles north of Stillwater, commuting distance from the Twin Cities.

The lake had risen more than ten feet that summer, bringing the water almost to the front deck. The owners had become discouraged by the constant threat of flooding and moved out, renting to us with a warning that we too might have to move at any time. The houses across the lake were already under water. We watched the lake rise a few more inches every day… until the water was five feet from the house. There it stopped.

For us, this was paradise. When standing under the cathedral ceilings in the living room, we looked out the picture window and saw water. It made us feel as if we were living on a houseboat.

* * *

We had only been living in the house for two months when a loud birdcall woke me at dawn. It was the last Saturday in September. Hoping the Canadian Geese had come for the cracked corn I had scattered on our shore to entice them, I felt a pang of disappointment when I saw a huge crow snatching up the kernels.

My intense connection to birds seemed forever broken. Wistfully I watched a red sun rise up like a giant balloon from behind the stand of pine trees across the lake. A Great Blue Heron sailed into view with his wings pressed against his sides, his long lean legs dangling straight out behind him, and his elegant neck tucked into a tight S-curve against his shoulders. He glided effortlessly while above him the sun drifted towards a bright blue sky.

It felt as though he had ushered in the day and what a gift of a day it was. Unusually warm, an Indian Summer day with the golden leaves on the elder tree glowing luminous in the sunlight; beside it, the little maple bush, a glorious contrast with its russet reds. The two of them alone could create fire.

Not only had the heron escorted in the day, he rekindled my hope that my connection to birds had not been severed irrevocably. You would think that after having so many marvelous experiences with birds, I would trust that they would always be in my life. The truth is, I feared the magic had already ended.

I never even stopped to wonder why I had so little faith.

* * *

Who should appear again that same day at dusk, and in time to carry his gift back to the nest, where he would sit on it like an egg, throughout the night, filling it with the magic of heron dreams?

The next day I spotted him again: a heron across the lake standing in the morning sunlight on the shore. With binoculars I could see him quite clearly. He spread his magnificent wings, lifted up into the air, and flew to the south end of the lake where he stood beside the driftwood, his feathers the exact same pale grey as the sun-bleached bark. I always wondered why he had been given the name Great Blue Heron, when he was so completely grey.

Once I knew that Lake Carnelian was one of his fishing spots, I started watching for the heron I now called Grey. Yet, it always surprised me when I actually spotted him.

Early one morning, I stepped out of my bathrobe and left it lying on the sand at the edge of the lake to take a swim. The water was bracing, but once I had been swimming for several minutes, I could feel the heat rise in my bones. From the middle of the lake I turned around to face the house and saw the heron standing on our shore right beside my robe. This time he was watching me with his little yellow eye. The way he looked at things reminded me of Lunker. The calm presence and the stillness he maintained for long periods of time brought back memories of Sadat. Like Hummer, he was much more distant and mysterious than any of the other birds I had known.

Often on my way into town, as I passed the green bog at the end of the south shore, I would see Grey perched on a dead stump. The moment he appeared, my heart skipped a beat.

I was always mesmerized by his mysterious presence. He made me feel as if I had been blessed.

Before long, I was spotting Grey several times a day. Sometimes I would watch a fisherman drifting right towards Grey without noticing him, my heron was standing so perfectly still, balanced on one leg on the sandbar or in the shallows. But Grey was always aware of everything around him. He would wait until the fisherman came within fifteen feet or so; then, in an instant, would spread his expansive wings, lift up from the ground, and without a sound fly off leisurely flapping his wings.

When he stood with his back to me, he looked like a snake rising out of the water. I couldn't see his beak at all; he had such a tiny head. With his wings folded tight against his body, he looked quite thin. Grey never ceased to intrigue me. While he stood on the shore, I don't think I ever saw him dip his beak into the water without pulling out a fish. He had incredible eyesight. I wondered sometimes what he saw when he looked at me. Surely he knew when I was there watching.

The Canadian Geese, the mallards, and a beautiful white swan had come and gone before the lake totally froze up a few days before Thanksgiving. Winter was coming fast but Grey hung around until every inch of the lake was frozen solid and he couldn't possibly pull out one more fish. Then he flew south. I wondered if he would make it back in the spring.

Even though we had a record snowfall and bitter cold winter that year, the white silence was glorious beside the lake. My biggest despair was that every day before sunrise I had to drive to work in St. Paul. I arrived back home after dark.

Once again, I was getting paid for typing someone else's words, the very thing I vowed never again to do when I left my first marriage. It seemed necessary though, to experience one more time the suffocation of my own creativity. It seemed the only way to force myself to trust my own voice enough to release it. And then, of course, there was the problem of making money with my writing.

Pierre and I decided to audition for the Minnesota Chautauqua. He wrote a couple of songs and taught me how to harmonize. Not an easy task, because I never trusted that I would hit the key. To our surprise we were chosen to perform in farming communities throughout Minnesota. I began practicing my flute and polishing up my poetry. We wanted to entertain them, to cheer them up, to celebrate those who truly love the land, care for it and preserve its beauty. Families who had owned the property for generations and loved every rock and tree felt an unfathomable failure when the bank foreclosed. There was a surge of suicide among the farmers.

We spent every spare moment that winter writing and rehearsing for our show.

CHAPTER 36

The Loon

Early that spring, we rushed off to Pierre's family farm for our very last visit. It had been sold and we had one last chance to walk the meadows, steam in the sauna, and swim in the clear waters of Long Lake.

In the Midwest, thousands of farms were being foreclosed and purchased by large corporations every month. We were witnessing a way of life disintegrate before our eyes. These struggling communities were the very places we would soon be performing in. The thought of it made me feel totally inadequate either to soothe their sorrows or to entertain them. Yet the grief we felt for losing the very place where we felt our spirits thrive gave us empathy for all the people who were losing their farms.

Long Lake was completely thawed, and we could smell spring in the air when Pierre and I began our last walk through the virgin pine forest his grandfather had planted. From the top of the hill you could look down any row and see the lake. We were gazing at the still water when we heard a loon calling from the middle of the lake.

His call brought back memories of all the summers we had spent in the cabin on the farm. Whenever we dipped our steaming bodies, hot from the sauna into the moonlit lake, the loon would call out, his mysterious sound echoing through the balmy night. Often we spent hours in silence listening for the loon.

On an impulse, I tried to imitate his sound. We listened to see if he would call again and heard nothing except a loud silence. Then a sound escaped my throat that surprised both of us in its similarity to the loon's rather hysterical call.

To my amazement, the loon responded. Pierre glanced at me in disbelief. Then we crouched down behind a tree, because the loon was swimming towards us. After I had exchanged seven calls with the loon, I began to feel overwhelmed with the thrill of it. Since Grey had flown south, I hadn't once connected with a bird. My emotions were playing havoc on my ability to focus; I didn't know whether to laugh or cry. Pierre nudged me, urging me to gather my composure and pay attention to the loon. He wanted me to take this opportunity as far as I could.

Before I had a chance to collect myself, the bird called again, this time adding new phrasing. Without thinking, I responded by imitating his previous call and realized my mistake immediately, as did he. By this time the loon was swimming up to the shoreline directly in front of the stand of pines we were hiding behind. There he glided back and forth searching for the bird who had answered his calls. When he didn't find her, he swam back to the middle of the lake.

We stood up, stretched our legs, and continued our walk marveling at the exchange.

I remember reading during my ornithological research that the mating rituals of birds have a very prescribed pattern and progression. If, at any point, either of the birds deviates from the sequence, the courting stops. When and if the calls resume, they must start again at the beginning.

As the sun began to set a few hours later, I watched the reflection of the pink and lavender clouds mirrored by the lake, and saw the loon swimming in front of the cabin about twenty feet from shore.

Oh, he's found me, I thought, absorbed by total belief in my miraculous connection to this bird. I made my way quickly down to the shore, and threw back my head. Full of confidence that I could imitate him, I cried out my most heart-felt loon call. He turned to look in my direction, but didn't respond.

His silence awakened me to the realization that he didn't have any connection to me in my human form the way Sadat, Hummer and Lunker had. No, it was my disembodied voice, sounding like the cry of a possible mate, that he had been attracted to. Now that I had revealed myself, he of course wasn’t interested.

Loons are such mysterious birds. They surface as if from the unconscious. Just when you are able to get a good look at them, they vanish. Their eerie call is like a laugh and at the same time a cry, containing in its parameters, the edges of both joy and madness. The loon offers us totality.

That night the sauna helped Pierre and me get down to the bare bones of our grief over losing the farm.

CHAPTER 37

Grey My Totem

Back on Lake Carnelian, I spotted a heron standing beside the driftwood. I wondered if he could possibly be Grey. This heron was so incredibly thin. Each time he dipped his beak into the water and pulled out a fish, I felt a tremendous relief that he might actually survive.

Within a month Grey looked the same size as when he had flown away the first of December.

Grey kept coming closer with every visit. When I was outside on the deck or digging in the flowerbeds next to the house, Grey would come within twenty feet or so. For hours he would stand staring into the water without moving, except for the one wispy feather on the back of his head that blew in the wind.

It was while I observed Grey that I wished I could somehow portray his magnificent presence. I was seeing Grey several times a day on our shore and taking it for granted that he would be in my life forever, when the landlord came to say that he had sold the house and we must move as soon as possible.

The day before we moved to a house in Stillwater, I was sitting on a blanket in the sand, trying to catch some sun while reading a magazine when a loud squawking noise startled me. It was Grey flying low overhead. He wanted me to see the smaller version of himself – his mate – flying close behind. Grey had never before made a sound. I wondered if he knew I was leaving.

In town I couldn't get Grey out of my thoughts. The intensity of my longing for him reminded me of my grief over losing Lunker. I wondered if losing the farm, the lake house, and Grey were just a few more lessons in letting go to prepare me for Jennifer's leaving home. Even though I knew such an independent young woman needed to create a space of her own, I grieved to see her go. Yet, at the same time I sensed that, with her departure, something new in me was about to be born.

I saw Grey while I was taking a walk along the St. Croix River and again when I went swimming at Square Lake. Soon I was seeing Grey almost every time I drove down Highway 36 to the Twin Cities. At first I thought it was the heron I had known at Lake Carnelian but soon realized that it no longer mattered if it was Grey or another Great Blue Heron. This bird had become my totem, and each time I saw him, I felt a rush of power.

While with the Minnesota Chautauqua traveling from town to town singing our songs and telling stories, I began for the first time to describe my relationship with Lunker. The farm people understood how one could love a creature so intensely. Often they rushed up after our show to share their stories of a bird or animal they had especially loved. Whenever

I looked out into the audience, I saw people who could have been the Scandinavian farmers of my childhood.

One night I looked down from the stage of a little town hall we were performing in. A farmer in the front row was cleaning his nails with a knife. The turkey wattle at his neck jiggled as he looked up and down.

I saw my grandfather and choked up so badly that Pierre had to finish the song alone. Fortunately, it was the last song of the evening.

We were to perform again the following day in Park Rapids, but that night in the motel, as I tried to fall asleep, memories of turkeys having the knife stuck in their throats kept recurring. I finally woke up in the middle of the night in a cold sweat from this dream:

> *In absolute terror, I was trying to pull a silver chain out of my throat. I knew at any moment I could choke to death, but at the same time I understood that it was essential to get out every last bit of the chain.*

Afterward I lay wide awake feeling certain that somehow I would never be able to sing again.

Just before we reached Park Rapids, I panicked. "I won't be able to sing. I don't know what's wrong."

"Stage fright," Pierre said. "It happens to everybody. Let's just stop the car here by the side of the road and take a little walk. You'll see. A little shot of sky and trees will calm you down."

We stopped by the river outside of town and stood on the banks beside the rushing water. I gazed at a tree limb being pulled under the water by a current. High up in the sky, I saw a heron flying by. I let out a long and ardent cry of delight and heard my voice return with more power than ever before. He swerved around, flew straight towards me, and glided past directly overhead. After we had watched him fly off and vanish in the distance, I sang the song we had written in honor of the grey heron, hoping he would hear me from afar.

As we stood on the riverbank, we sang through every song in our repertoire with such joy as I had never felt before. Then we drove on to Park Rapids and gave one of our best performances ever.

Among the farm families, I rediscovered my voice – the kind of carefree, fearless voice I had lost as a child while swallowing my horror at the sight of the turkey slaughter.

Without the birds who came to my rescue, my story would still be stuck in my throat.

Acknowledgements

I give thanks to Pierre Delattre for our many wonderful years of a shared creative life. While we lived in Mexico, the synchronistic relationships with birds took place. I feel blessed by his enthusiasm for all our writing and painting endeavors. For me, there couldn't be a better companion.

I am grateful for my two beautiful daughters, Carla and Jennifer, who are major characters in my life story. They both continue to teach me about courage and compassion.

I give thanks to Nor Hall for her careful reading of the book and her extraordinary wordsmith talent; to Milne Kintner for her coaching brilliance and encouragement, to Michele Delattre for her story-line insights and creation of the audio, and to Stephanie Carnes for her design skills and technical support.

Left to right: Jennifer with Little Guy, Nancy with Big Lunker, Carla and Pierre, 1980. Photo: Don Wolf.